النجـوم السـاطعـة مـن اصـحاب النـبي ﷺ

SHINING STARS

Among the Prophet's Companions

Vol. 1

First Edition: May 2001

Printed in Lebanon

Supervised by:
ABDUL MALIK MUJAHID

Headquarters:

P.O. Box: 22743, Riyadh 11416, KSA
Tel: 00966-1-4033962/4043432
Fax:00966-1- 4021659
E-mail: darussalam@naseej.com.sa
Website: http:// www.dar-us-salam.com
Bookshop: Tel & Fax: 00966-1-4614483

Branches & Agents:

K.S. A.

- Jeddah: Tel & Fax: 00966-2-6807752
- Al-Khobar: Tel & Fax: 00966-3-8692900

U.A.E.

- Tel: 00971-6-5511293 Fax: 5511294

PAKISTAN

- 50 Lower Mall, Lahore
  Tel: 0092-42-724 0024 Fax: 7354072
- Rahman Market, Ghazni Street
  Urdu Bazar, Lahore
  Tel: 0092-42-7120054 Fax: 7320703

U. S. A.

- Houston: P.O. Box: 79194 Tx 77279
  Tel: 001-713-722 0419 Fax: 001-713-722 0431
  E-mail: Sales @ dar-us-salam.com
  Website: http:// www.dar-us-salam.com
- New York: 572 Atlantic Ave, Brooklyn
  New York-11217
  Tel: 001-718-625 5925

U.K.

- London: Darussalam International Publications Ltd.
  P.O. Box: 21555, London E10 6XQ
  Tel: 044-7947 306 706 Fax: 0044-208 925 6996
- Birmingham: Al-Hidaayah Publishing & Distribution
  436 Coventry Road, Birmingham B10 OUG
  Tel: 0044-121-753 1889 Fax: 121-753 2422

AUSTRALIA

- Lakemba NSW: ICIS: Ground Floor 165-171, Haldon St.
  Tel: (61-2) 9758 4040 Fax: 9758 4030

MALAYSIA

- E&D BOOKS SDN.BHD.-321 B 3rd Floor, Suria Klcc
  Kuala Lumpur City Center 50088
  Tel: 00603-21663433 Fax: 459 72032

SINGAPORE

- Muslim Converts Association of Singapore
  Singapore- 424484
  Tel: 0065-440 6924, 348 8344 Fax: 440 6724

SRI LANKA

- Darul Kitab 6, Nirmal Road, Colombo-4
  Tel: 0094-1-589 038 Fax: 0094-74 722433

KUWAIT

- Islam Presentation Committee
  Enlightment Book Shop
  P.O. Box : 1613, Safat 13017 KUWAIT
  Tel: 00965-244 7526, Fax: 240 0057

BANGLADESH

- 30 Malitola Road, Dhaka-1100
  Tel: 0088-02-9557214, Fax: 0088-02-9559738

SHINING STARS

Among the Prophet's Companions

Vol. 1

By
Abdul Basit Ahmad
Edited by
Muhammad Ayub Sipra

DARUSSALAM
GLOBAL LEADER IN ISLAMIC BOOKS
Riyadh • Jeddah • Sharjah • Lahore
London • Houston • New York

In the Name of Allâh,
the Most Gracious, the Most Merciful

Contents

Publishers Note

All praises are due to Allâh, the Lord of all that exists. May Allâh's peace and blessings be upon His final Prophet and Messenger, Muhammad, his family and his Companions.

Darussalam is pleased to present this valuable book, 'Shining Stars among the Prophet's Companions', in two volumes. The purpose of this book is to enlighten our youth about the lives of the greatest Companions of the Prophet ﷺ. Also, we wish to increase the enthusiasm of the Muslim youth for following and adhering to their religion. In this way, these books achieve two very important tasks: educating our youth and encouraging them to be good Muslims.

First volume is in your hands. You will see that the author has selected the nine top rank Companions of the Prophet ﷺ. Although these were all given the good news of Paradise even then they played an active role in their life till the last.

They are humble, just, tender and dedicated to the support of the Prophet ﷺ and Islam. Their rank among the Companions was very high to the extent that the Prophet ﷺ told them that they were given the good news of Paradise.

In the description of the lives of the Companions, we find example for ourselves and our youth as to how they strictly followed the laws and commandments of Islam and how they loved the Prophet ﷺ so greatly that they did not hesitated to offer their lives and their wealth for the safety of the Prophet ﷺ and for Islam. They took each and every saying of the Prophet ﷺ and his act to be a guiding principle for their whole life. If we learn about them and try to follow them in this respect no wonder that Allâh would help us and our youth with sound faith, uprightness and ease to follow their path and attain nearness to Allâh.

We hope that this book is beneficial to our Muslim youth, as they are the future of Islam. We, at Darussalam realize the importance of good Islamic literature for Muslim youth, especially in the West where non-Islamic influences are so strong. For this reason, we feel that the availability of this book will be a valuable aid in instilling a genuine love for Islam in our youth. We would like to thank the author, Mr. Abdul Basit Ahmad, the editor Mr. Muhammad Ayub Sipra for their diligent work in preparing this series. As Allâh says:

"Is there any reward for good other than good?" (55:60)

And our final invocation is that all praises are due to Allâh, the Lord of all that exists.

Abdul Malik Mujahid
General Manager

Foreword

Most, if not all, human beings would think twice before accepting any idea or belief. They usually like to see evidences of the truth of the idea that they are called to accept. While thinking whether to accept or reject any idea, many factors either bring them closer to or drive them far from the idea proposed to them. If such factors that are usually connected with the idea are sensible then there is the collective acceptance of it by the society.

To accept an idea from the first instance means that the person invited to such an idea either already knows much about the person who calls him to believe in what he is saying, or he feels the sensibility of the idea compared to the contradictions prevailing in the society, or has a power of intellect and high mentality that distinguishes him from other members of the society and he can well judge the truth or the falseness of it by himself.

Any preacher might have many followers who seek to learn the teachings of religion from him. However, few of them truly understand the themes that the preacher was teaching them. A student might have something that interferes with his learning. Another one might not be fully interested in the knowledge given to him and hence loses most of the things he learnt from his teacher. However, there are followers who dedicate all their time and efforts to gaining as much knowledge as they can. Not only this, but also they follow every act and deed of their teacher. They cling to their teacher's directions under all conditions.

In this concise biography, we are going to have a look at the lives of the Companions of the Prophet Muhammad ﷺ who were great examples of devout followers. As a result of their keen dedication, they became the most prominent leaders of Islam.

Before accepting the call of a new religion, our heroes, belonged to good and humble families but they were worshipping idols of stones, elements of nature or other human beings. With the progress of the Islamic call, they became true believers who never hesitated to provide all support to the Prophet ﷺ and the religion of Islam. They sacrificed all they had for the sake of spreading the call of the new religion.

Even when they were elected as a Caliph or commander of the Muslim army, they continued the same course of life they had before. They worked sincerely for Islam and never had rest until they were sure that Islam had been deeply rooted in the Arab society and other societies as well.

Let us together go through the following stories to know about these great Companions of the Prophet ﷺ who played a major role in building the future of Islam.

Abdul Basit Ahmad

Introduction

The Prophet's Companions

The Arab society in the Arabian Peninsula and surrounding areas mainly consisted of tribes and clans. Some of them lived in towns while most of them followed their flocks everywhere in the desert in search of food and water. These tribes were usually involved in wars amongst each other. Every tribe was invading and invaded by other tribes. The gloom that loomed over the Arabian Peninsula and the world in general before the rise of Islam killed nearly every virtue in the minds and hearts of human beings at that time. Human rights, for example, were not given any value. Slavery, burying girls alive and injustices were dominating the societies of the city and desert alike. Youth and old were spending their time in grazing animals or practicing trade during the daytime and seeking trivial pleasures during the night. The guidance brought by previous religions was absent from the life of people. There was no central government; rather, every tribe had its own chief and customs in spite of the fact that some common laws were prevailing in the society. The people of Arabia were largely idol worshippers. A number of Jews and Christians were scattered here and there, but their practice of their religions had greatly diminished. Every Arab tribe had its own deities and its own forms of worship. The Ka'bah in Makkah was itself surrounded with hundreds of idols which were considered by Makkans as gods.

All these vices and atrocities urgently needed a Messenger from Allâh to reform the society and spread guidance throughout the Arabian Peninsula in particular and the world in general. When the Prophet ﷺ began calling Arabs to accept the message of Islam, few people, mostly weak slaves, accepted Islam and received much oppression for holding to their faith. Within twenty-three years, Islam spread over Arabia. The people who accepted the message of Islam and met the Prophet ﷺ were named by the Prophet ﷺ himself as his Companions. Under the light of Islam they changed from idolaters to sources of light and wisdom to the whole world.

A Prophet's Companion is defined as a person who believed in the Prophet ﷺ and came in contact with him. The Prophet ﷺ told about believers to come (in the future) and called them as his "brothers". The Companions of the Prophet ﷺ exclaimed:

"Are not we your brothers?"

The Prophet ﷺ told them:

"You are my Companions. My brothers are those who would believe in me although they did not see me."

Seniority of the Prophet's Companions depended on their initiative to accept Islam, emigration to Al-Madinah and participation in the battle of Badr. Allâh confirmed this classification by placing the early Muslims of migrants and supporters on the top of the list of believers. Hence, one cannot say that those who accepted Islam after the conquest of Makkah were equal to Abu Bakr رضي الله عنه or Bilal رضي الله عنه in rank. Abu Bakr and Bilal رضي الله عنهما were among the first people who accepted Islam. They spent all their resources for the sake of Islam and emigrated with the Prophet ﷺ to Al-Madinah. They participated in Badr and all battles of Islam against idolatry. Allâh stated in the Qur'ân that those who emigrated after the conquest of Makkah are not equal to those who emigrated before it. 'Umar bin Al-Khattab ﷺ once received a group of the Prophet's Companions. He gave priority to Bilal ﷺ over Abu Sufyan ﷺ and others. Some people protested to such an act. Those waiting to meet the Caliph replied that Bilal ﷺ accepted Islam when he (Abu Sufyan) fought against it. The Prophet ﷺ said:

"The best people are those who live at my time (meaning his Companions), followed by those who come after them and the ones who come after the latter."

Therefore, we hold all of the Prophet's Companions to be good and we do not prefer some while hate others. Some of the Prophet's Companions were foretold by the Prophet ﷺ that they would dwell in Paradise in the Hereafter. Also, the Four Rightly Guided Caliphs of Islam are placed first on the list of the Companions of the Prophet as they combined many characteristics that no other Companions had. Some people of our time ignorantly criticize the Companions of the Prophet ﷺ. He ﷺ said:

"Do not say anything bad about my Companions..."

Therefore, we should respect all Companion of the Prophet ﷺ. We should also believe that they were the best men created by Allâh after the Prophets. They led a life of piety and devotion and followed the steps of the Prophet ﷺ. They were the living models of the teachings of the Qur'ân. They lived during the period that the Qur'ân was being revealed to the Prophet ﷺ and applied it in letter and spirit to their lives. They sacrificed all their resources to support the Word of Allâh. When you will read about them you will discover something new about their dedication and truthfulness. Abu Bakr ﷺ, for example, was told by the Quraish that the Prophet ﷺ claimed to have been taken by Allâh on a journey during one night to Al-Aqsa Mosque in Palestine. He immediately believed in what the Prophet ﷺ had said. He replied to those who doubted that journey:

> "I believed in what he said is a revelation from heaven (the Qur'ân). Why should I not believe in something that he claimed to have taken place on earth?"

'Umar bin Al-Khattab رضي الله عنه was a bright example of justice and humility. He feared for anyone under his rule to be treated badly, whether a Muslim or a non-Muslim. He used to go from place to place in Al-Madinah during the night to be sure that the nation was in a good condition. He once saw a fire at the outskirts of the city. When he approached, he saw a woman with her children crying for food. When he found out that they had no food, he returned to the state treasury, took some food, carried it on his shoulders and cooked it for the woman and her children. He feared that he might be punished on the Day of Judgment for any injustice done to the people. 'Uthman bin 'Affan رضي الله عنه was so bashful that the Prophet ﷺ said that angels feel bashful when they see 'Uthman رضي الله عنه. He received a caravan loaded with all kinds of food when the people were suffering a famine. Merchants offered him five times the price of his goods but he refused to sell to them. He told them that he donated the goods to the people of Al-Madinah. 'Ali bin Abi Tâlib رضي الله عنه was the first boy to believe in the Prophet ﷺ. He was even ready to sacrifice his life for the life of the Prophet ﷺ when the Quraish wanted to murder the Prophet ﷺ. He slept in the Prophet's bed on the night when the Prophet ﷺ emigrated to Al-Madinah in order to misguide the pagans. He was the husband of Fatimah رضي الله عنها, the Prophet's daughter and the purest woman on earth. Az-Zubair bin Al-'Awwam رضي الله عنه, whom the Prophet ﷺ called "his disciple", Talhah bin 'Ubaidullah ﷺ, who risked his life to defend the Prophet ﷺ at the battle of Uhud and Sa'd bin Abi Waqqas ﷺ, who was a man whom the Prophet ﷺ was proud to have as his uncle, all are live examples of the sincerity and dedication that the Companions of the Prophet ﷺ exercised toward their faith. Then there was Salman Al-Farisi ﷺ, who toured the world in quest of truth. Suhaib Ar-Roomi ﷺ surrendered all of his money to the pagans so that they would allow him to join the Prophet ﷺ and his fellow Muslims in Al-Madinah. Khalid bin Al-Waleed and Abu 'Ubaidah bin Al-Jarrah رضي الله عنهما led the Muslim armies beyond the borders of Arabia to spread the light of Islam all over the world. These and many others of the Companions of the Prophet ﷺ were the people who taught us how true Muslims should be. These were the Companions of the Prophet ﷺ to whom we are greatly indebted, for had it not been for their sacrifices and devotion, we would not have been Muslims today. Therefore, I would like to ask my readers to say رضي الله عنهم (may Allâh be pleased with them) whenever they read or hear their names. Allâh told us in the Qur'ân that he was pleased with them and He selected them to be the Companions of the Prophet ﷺ and the most qualified people to spread His Word.

ابو بكر الصديق رضي الله عنه

— أول الخلفاء الراشدين —

Abu Bakr As-Siddiq رضي الله عنه

The First Caliph of Islam

Background

Abu Bakr was born in Makkah two years after the birth of the Prophet ﷺ. His parents belonged to a clan called Banu Taim, a branch from the Quraish tribe. The boy was brought up in an environment characterized by excellence of chivalry, generosity and manliness.

In the period before Islam, this clan was assigned a function that made it well established within the Makkan society. Blood money in murder cases was referred to Abu Bakr's father who in turn assigned the job to his son.

Before conversion to Islam, Abu Bakr was well known for his excellent manners, wide knowledge and perfect wisdom. He was consulted on important matters and his decision was always final. He was even considered the greatest authority of his day on matters related to relations among clans and tribes.

After he converted to Islam, the Prophet ﷺ named him Abdullah instead of his previous name Abdul Ka'bah. He was popularly known among people as Abu Bakr followed by a quality that the most Companions of the Prophet ﷺ confirmed it was given to him by Allâh through the Prophet ﷺ. That quality was 'As-Siddiq' (the most truthful). He was also given another quality by the Prophet ﷺ which was Al-'Ateeq (the liberated) from Hellfire.

Abu Bakr ﷺ was a successful merchant and was highly respected for his fair dealings. All society members knew about his high morals and fine treatment of slavs.

Conversion to Islam

Relation to the Prophet ﷺ

Abu Bakr lived in the same neighborhood where the Prophet ﷺ lived. Before the Prophet ﷺ was twenty-five years old, no contacts were made between him and Abu Bakr. However, it was clear that both the Prophet ﷺ and Abu Bakr became close friends after that time. They were nearly of the same age, their natures were uniform, both of them abhorred the corrupt beliefs and practices of the Quraish and both of them kept themselves away from the evil habits of the day. Hence, Abu Bakr became the most trusted man and a confidant of the Prophet ﷺ.

The first Muslim

After he was ordered to preach the new religion, the Prophet ﷺ invited Abu Bakr to accept the new faith. Abu Bakr did not avoid him or ask him to give him time to think it over. The Prophet ﷺ said:

> "Whenever I invited anyone to accept Islam, he argued with me and rejected my words at the outset except the son of Abu Quhafa (Abu Bakr). He accepted it immediately and stayed steadfast in it."

At the beginning of the call, Abu Bakr ﷺ was on a trade journey in Yemen. On his return to Makkah, some chiefs of the

Quraish came to see him. They told him that Muhammad ﷺ had declared himself to be the Prophet. They were waiting for his return to help them find ways to stop the call. Instead of plotting with them against the Prophet ﷺ, Abu Bakr hurried to the Prophet ﷺ, asked him about the Divine Message and immediately accepted Islam at the very meeting with the Prophet ﷺ. Abu Bakr did not have any doubts about the themes presented by the Prophet ﷺ. He directly believed the claims of the Prophet ﷺ of an angel (Gabriel) bringing down revelation to him from Allâh. He knew from the very beginning that worshipping idols had been an act of silliness. On the other hand, he recognized the truthfulness, honesty, nobility and piety of the Prophet ﷺ. Hence, he, from the first instance, supported his Massage because it satisfied the demands of his reason and soul.

Thus, Abu Bakr ﷺ was destined to be the first believer of Islam. His zeal for upholding truth, right and justice prepared him to make great sacrifices and face many hardships. Moreover, his approach in convincing others of the truth of Islam brought so many to the fold of Islam. He used up his wealth to free slaves who converted to Islam and to save them from the agonies and oppression, which the Quraish inflicted on them. He, himself, suffered a lot at the hands of the tyrants, so much so that he was left once unconscious after he was beaten to near death. It did not bother him for his wealth to be used up for the sake of Allâh and the propagation of the new light of Islam.

The true Believer

In every test of oppression, Abu Bakr ﷺ gave firm proof of

his firm faith. He did not expect any material gains from his support of Islam. His protection of converts saved them from the mischievous acts of the Quraish and provided them with a shelter to worship Allâh in relative peace.

Emigration to Al-Madinah

Desperate Efforts

No doubt that the way the Prophet ﷺ preached his message for thirteen years in Makkah had no parallel in history. His courage and determination in the face of bitter opposition will always be a source of inspiration to those who work in the cause of Truth and Justice. He began single handed with no visible means of protection to meet the attacks of the barbarous tribes of Arabia. It was really a difficult mission to change those people, who were notorious for their worship of idols and criminal acts, into clean and civilized human beings.

Side by side with the Prophet ﷺ

The assistance provided by Abu Bakr ﷺ in helping the cause and protecting weak converts created a strong bond between him and the Prophet ﷺ. This bond was further confirmed by their joint departure to Al-Madinah.

Change of Direction

As the Prophet ﷺ felt desperate to change the society of Makkah, he decided to address those who came from afar to participate in fairs outside the city. On many occasions, the response was negative in the beginning. But soon the Prophet ﷺ happened to see a group of visitors from Yathrib. They listened to his message on the very first occasion and in the course of a couple of years a number of them accepted the Islamic Faith.

Protection Attained

The Prophet ﷺ caught this chance to provide his Companions with a place of security. He already had held a pledge of protection with the chiefs of Yathrib. Hence, the Prophet ﷺ permitted his Companions to start emigrating to Yathrib. He himself was preparing to leave the city to the new place where he could find peace to preach the Message. His Companions began emigrating to Yathrib in batches and groups until most of them left the city under the cover of darkness leaving behind their houses and property.

First in Everything

Abu Bakr ﷺ himself expressed his wish on many occasions to leave Yathrib but the Prophet ﷺ was always asking him to wait for a while. The Prophet ﷺ said to him:

> "Do not do so yet. May be Allâh will send a companion to be with you when you emigrate."

These words gave Abu Bakr ﷺ a strong feeling that the Prophet ﷺ would be his companion. At the same time, he was afraid lest the Quraish would come to know that the Prophet ﷺ was planning to leave Makkah.

Four months had now passed since the first batches of Muslims had left Makkah. There were only a few people who for one reason or another could not leave the city including the Prophet ﷺ, Abu Bakr and 'Ali bin Abi Tâlib رضي الله عنهما

The plot to murder the Prophet ﷺ

The Quraish felt the danger of permitting the Muslims to

escape their control. Hence, they finally decided to put an end to the Prophet's life. They agreed to have about forty young men from all tribes to stand by the house of the Prophet ﷺ one night and tear his body with their swords.

Orders to Emigrate to Al-Madinah

The Prophet ﷺ, however, was informed by Allâh of the plot and was instructed to emigrate. The Prophet ﷺ in turn told his close friend, Abu Bakr ؓ, to be ready for the sacred voyage. Abu Bakr ؓ had already bought two camels to use in his journey to Al-Madinah. He had fed the two camels well in preparation for the long journey.

Leaving the Homeland

Early morning before dawn, the Prophet ﷺ ordered his cousin, 'Ali ؓ, to cover himself with his blanket and sleep in his bed. The Prophet ﷺ left, passing in front of the youth surrounding his house. He reached the house of Abu Bakr ؓ who kept awake and ready to join the Prophet ﷺ. They both made for the cave of Thaur about five miles south of Makkah.

In the Cave

Both the Prophet ﷺ and Abu Bakr ؓ kept in the cave while Makkans were searching everywhere to find the two emigrants after they had discovered that the Prophet ﷺ had escaped them. The Quraish horsemen came very close to the cave and Abu Bakr ؓ felt his body shivering for fear of being seen by pursuers. However the Prophet ﷺ whispered in his ear:

"Be not sad (or afraid), surely, Allâh is with us." (9:40)

The pursuers came very close to the mouth of the cave and

would have seen the Prophet ﷺ and his Companion had they gone into that cave. But thanks to Allâh they left in dismay and the Prophet ﷺ and his Companion kept safe. They were very sure that Allâh had protected them.

Sacrifices for the Prophet ﷺ

In fact, Abu Bakr ﷺ feared for the Prophet's life more than he feared for his own life. As soon as both men arrived at the cave, Abu Bakr ﷺ asked the Prophet ﷺ to stay outside. He went inside to check the cave. He knew that if the Quraish had got hold of the Prophet ﷺ, it would have been the end of Islam. He had already proved his dedication to the safety of the Prophet ﷺ and the message of Islam.

Both men spent three days in the cave until the Quraish's search cooled down. They were served every night with food by Abu Bakr's daughter, Asma' رضي الله عنها and brought news of the search efforts by Abu Bakr's son, Abdur-Rahman ﷺ.

The Reward

Because the Quraish were not able to catch the Prophet ﷺ and his Companion, they fixed a reward of one hundred camels for whoever caught hold of the two migrants. The Prophet ﷺ, Abu Bakr ﷺ, a guide and a servant left the cave and headed to Al-Madinah on zigzagging ways to mislead the pagans.

Attempts to catch the two Emigrants

On the way to Al-Madinah, a horseman named Suraqah bin Malik followed the emigrants. Suraqah heard news of the reward set by the Quraish for the heads of the Prophet ﷺ and Abu Bakr ﷺ. The man got very near to them and was about to get hold of them. Abu Bark ﷺ told the Prophet ﷺ

that someone had been following their steps. The Prophet ﷺ calmly prayed to Allâh to save them. No sooner did the Prophet ﷺ finish his supplication, the horseman was thrown down from his horse. He tried again to catch the Prophet ﷺ and his Companion, but once more his horse's feet went deep in the sand and could not move a step forward. Once more, the horseman did his best to come near the group of travelers, but his horse fell down and he was thrown off its back. Now he knew that the Prophet ﷺ and his Companion were out of his reach and that they were true in their Faith. He shouted to the Prophet ﷺ and his Companion asking them to forgive him and promised them to go back and even to mislead other reward seekers. The Prophet ﷺ prayed to Allâh to forgive the man.

Signs of Prophethood

As the Prophet ﷺ and his Companion felt safe, they sought some rest and food. They stopped at a tent known to Arabs on the way to Al-Madinah. There lived a woman named Umm Ma'abad with her sheep. She was selling milk and food to travelers. Abu Bakr ﷺ asked her to sell them some milk. She complained that she had no milk to sell. The Prophet ﷺ saw a very weak sheep beside the tent. He asked the woman permission to milk it. She did not object although she was sure the sheep would not give any drop of milk. The Prophet ﷺ prayed to Allâh, touched the sheep's breast and began milking it. To the woman's astonishment, he milked a full pot. He took some sips of milk, gave the pot to Abu Bakr ﷺ and the other two men to drink. All of them got enough milk and left the rest for the woman.

The people welcome the Prophet ﷺ

News of the departure of the Prophet ﷺ and his Companion from Makkah reached Al-Madinah. They were expected to arrive on a certain day. All the people in Al-Madinah were waiting at the outskirts of the town for there arrival. On the day of the arrival, men, women and children were waiting under the heat of the sun until it was high noon. They were about to leave back to their homes but a Jew called them from the top of a palm tree telling them to wait. He told them that the emigrants for whom they were waiting appeared in the horizon. The inhabitants of Al-Madinah and early emigrants felt happy for the safe arrival of the Prophet ﷺ and his Companion. They welcomed the group with cheers of joy and praises to Allâh.

Covenants with the Jews

During this period, the Prophet ﷺ, Abu Bakr ﷺ and other Muslims did their best to foster relations with the Jews. Jews were settling in the suburbs of Al-Madinah. The Prophet ﷺ held with them a pact of mutual support. However, the Jews did not respect their covenants on several occasions. Threats from other tribes, especially from the Quraish in Makkah, were increasing. Day after day, the Muslims felt the need to strengthen their forces in order to stand fast against the forces of evil.

Challenges to the Message of Islam

The Muslim settled in Al-Madinah under the protection of the *Ansâr*. But the Quraish forced and threatened the Polytheist of Al-Madinah to provide help to them against Muslims. Upon this Allâh allowed the Muslims to fight the Quraish in self-defense. The Muslims began patrolling ouside Al-Madinah for security purposes. They received the news of a Quraish caravan nearby. They went towards it to check it. Abu Sufyan, the loader of the caravan, got the news of Muslims coming towards them, in fear of their attack, he changed his direction and managed to escape. He also sent a warning massage to the Quraish that their trade caravan was in danger. But when he felt safe, he sent another man to deliver good news to the Quraish about the caravan. However, Abu Jahl, a leader of the Quraish and a bitter enemy of the Prophet ﷺ and Islam, insisted on putting an end to any future threat from Muslims. He convinced other chiefs to march to Al-Madinah to destroy Muslims and Islam.

Preparations for Combat

The Quraish deployed a strong army and marched to Al-Madinah. The Muslims, on the other hand, did not have enough provisions for the coming battle. However, they were determined to stop the aggressors.

Badr Battle: the Quraish are Defeated

The Prophet ﷺ with the help of Abu Bakr ﷺ and other Muslim leaders gathered an army one-third the number of the Quraish army. Both armies met at a place called Badr. There the Prophet ﷺ was provided with a shelter and guarded by Abu Bakr ﷺ to manage the battle. Abu Bakr ﷺ was standing behind the Prophet ﷺ while he was praying to Allâh to grant the Muslims victory over the disbelievers. Many times did the Prophet's cloak fall off his shoulders and Abu Bakr ﷺ picked it up. He was close to the Prophet ﷺ when he was praying:

"O Allâh! If this small band is defeated, no one on earth will worship You."

As the Prophet ﷺ received reassurance from above, he commanded the Muslims to start action.

Throughout the battle, Abu Bakr ﷺ remained by the side of the Prophet ﷺ. He was again and again encouraging the Prophet ﷺ by words like:

"O Prophet of Allâh (ﷺ) ! Why fear? Allâh has promised to you victory and support. He certainly will fulfil His Word."

Witness to Allâh's Help

No sooner did the battle become hot than the Prophet ﷺ told Abu Bakr ﷺ that help of Allâh had come. He said to him:

"Here is Gabriel عليه السلام riding a horse with its reins in hand and dust on its teeth."

The volunteers of Islam won the much needed and much deserved victory. They took seventy soldiers of the Quraish army as captives. Some of these captives were eminent and even closely related to the Prophet ﷺ. These were the same people who had oppressed the Muslims as much as they could and made their life in Makkah impossible. They expected that the Prophet ﷺ would take revenge on them. Therefore, they wanted to talk to Abu Bakr ﷺ. He promised to help them. The Prophet ﷺ accepted the counsel of Abu Bakr ﷺ and agreed to take ransom from some of the captives and release many others who could not pay.

The new Challenges

The victory of Badr opened a new page in the history of Islam and Muslims. The Prophet ﷺ began planning future actions. The Jews and the surrounding tribes were not happy with this victory. Grudge and anger made them join hands against Muslims. In the face of such dangers, the Prophet ﷺ was always consulting Abu Bakr ؓ and other Companions from both emigrants and supporters to create a sense of unity among all Muslims.

The Jews did not hesitate to announce their jealousy and plans to defeat the cause of Muslims. They began harassing the Muslims through plots to weaken them. One Jewish clan named Banu Qaynuqa‘, went very far in harming the Muslims. The Prophet ﷺ had no choice but to make them leave their land to keep their plots away from the Muslims.

Uhud Battle

The Quraish, on the other hand, did not give up the idea of taking revenge for their defeat at the battle of Badr. They collected a well-equipped army and marched near to Uhud Mount in the vicinity of Al-Madinah. Abu Bakr ؓ and some other Companions of the Prophet ﷺ played a major part in preventing the Quraish from achieving any gain from the partial defeat of the Muslims. He and his brothers in Islam stood fast and protected the Prophet ﷺ. Abu Bakr ؓ was second to none in fighting the Quraish and protecting the life of the Prophet ﷺ in this battle.

Battle of the Trench

As the Quraish were not satisfied with the results of the Uhud

Battle. They plotted with the Jews and other tribes of Arabia called the 'confederates' to fight their last and deadly battle against the Muslims. With an army numbering ten thousand soldiers, they marched toward Al-Madinah to loot through the city and put an end to Islam and the Muslims. The Jews, on the other hand, sent secret messages to the Quraish that they would stand by their side against the Muslims.

The Muslims were not well prepared for this battle. They were well aware that if the Quraish army was allowed to occupy the town of Al-Madinah, they would destroy the whole message of Islam. The Prophet ﷺ, Abu Bakr ﷺ and other Companions counsel the best way to stop the attack. Finally, a Companion named Salman Al-Farisi ﷺ, originally from Persia, proposed to dig a trench around weak points of Al-Madinah to deter the attackers. The last attempt by the Quraish to kill Islam in its cradle was successfully foiled by this military trick which the Arabs had not seen before.

The Hudaibiyah Peace Agreement

After the Trench Battle, the Prophet ﷺ, Abu Bakr ﷺ and other Companions wished to visit Makkah. Fourteen hundred Muslims, barely armed, marched to Makkah. The were stopped by the Quraish at a place called Hudaibiyah close to Makkah. Finally a peace agreement was held between the Muslims and the Quraish stating that the Muslims should go back this year and come back next year for three days only. The Prophet ﷺ, supported by Abu Bakr ﷺ, accepted the agreement. The next year, Abu Bakr ﷺ was ordered by the Prophet ﷺ to lead the Muslims on their trip to make pilgrimage.

Conquest of Makkah

The Quraish did not keep its word according to the Hudaibiyah peace agreement. They attacked a tribe that held alliance with the Muslims and killed some of them. The Prophet ﷺ and his Companions were now released from the obligations of the agreement. The Prophet ﷺ, as promised by Allâh, marched to Makkah at the head of an army of ten thousand soldiers. The Prophet ﷺ announced that the people of Makkah would be safe and secure if they did not challenge the advancing army. Anyone who kept inside his house or resorted to the Ka'bah would not be taken as a foe. The Prophet ﷺ, Abu Bakr ﷺ and the Muslims conquered Makkah peacefully. There, the Prophet ﷺ declared clearly and loudly that all past enemies are free and none should harm them.

The Farewell Pilgrimage

Soon after conquering Makkah, the Prophet ﷺ decided to perform *Hajj* (pilgrimage). One hundred thousand Muslims accompanied the Prophet ﷺ to the blessed land to perform pilgrimage. Abu Bakr ﷺ was beside the Prophet ﷺ when he stood at Arafat announcing that the religion of Islam was now complete and perfect. Abu Bakr ﷺ was so happy to hear these words from the Prophet ﷺ. However, at the same time, he felt very sad for he knew that the end of the Prophet's life had come close.

The Prophet ﷺ falls Ill

A short period after performing pilgrimage, the Prophet ﷺ fell ill. Abu Bakr ﷺ was very afraid to lose company with the Prophet ﷺ. During his illness, the Prophet ﷺ came into the mosque, ascended the pulpit and said:

> "Allâh offered to His servant (the Prophet ﷺ) the privilege of choosing this world or the Hereafter. The servant chose the Hereafter to be close to Allâh."

Abu Bakr ﷺ understood what the Prophet's statement implied. He began weeping bitterly. He asked:

> "O Prophet of Allâh ﷺ! Our lives and children be sacrificed for you. How would we live after you."

During his address, the Prophet ﷺ ordered all doors leading to the mosque to be closed except the door of Abu Bakr ﷺ. He added pointing to Abu Bakr ﷺ:

> "I found no one best among my Companions other than Abu Bakr ﷺ. However my relation with Abu Bakr is that of a close friend, Islamic brotherhood and Faith until Allâh raises us together."

The leader of Prayers

During the Prophet's illness, Abu Bakr ﷺ was leading the prayers. In the *Fajr* (Dawn) prayer, the Prophet ﷺ came in the mosque supported by two of his Companions. Abu Bakr ﷺ was leading the prayer. The Companions of the Prophet ﷺ were so happy to see the Prophet ﷺ. Abu Bakr ﷺ gave way for the Prophet ﷺ to lead the prayer. However, the Prophet ﷺ ordered Abu Bakr ﷺ to continue as leading the prayer and sat to Abu Bakr's side and offered prayer. As the Prophet ﷺ completed his prayer, he came back to his house where he felt very sick. After a while his blessed soul ascended to the heavens.

Wise and Balanced Muslim

Abu Bakr ﷺ, unlike other Muslims who were shocked by the news, entered to where the Prophet ﷺ was lying, kissed his face and said:

"My father and mother be a sacrifice for you. You are good while alive and as dead."

Some Companions threatened anyone who would say that the Prophet ﷺ had died. Abu Bakr ﷺ came out stressing the fact that no one would live forever even the Prophet ﷺ. Now, all the Companions understood the reality and accepted the fact. So, Abu Bakr ﷺ controlled the situation and brought the people out of confusion. He saved the Muslim community from total disruption.

Abu Bakr ﷺ did not forget in this grave situation that Allâh told the Prophet ﷺ in the Qur'ân:

"Verily you will die, and Verily, they (too) will die." (39:30)

Abu Bakr ﷺ selected as Caliph (ruler)

Selection of the Caliph

Immediately after the Prophet ﷺ passed away, his prominent Companions met to choose a successor. At a place called Saqifah, Abu Bakr ﷺ was distinguished to be the man rightly suitable for the position. After lengthy discussions, 'Umar bin Al-Khattab and Abu 'Ubaidah bin Al-Jarrah رضي الله عنهما held the hand of Abu Bakr ﷺ and announced him as the Caliph (ruler). All people, both emigrants and supporters supported electing Abu Bakr ﷺ as a Caliph. On the next day, most people came to the mosque to pledge obedience to Abu Bakr ﷺ.

Abu Bakr ﷺ ascended the pulpit and expressed his sorrow for the Prophet's departure from this world. He added:

> "O people! I swear by Allâh that I never wanted to be a Caliph or wished to be so. It is a big task that you put on my shoulders. Obey me as long as I obey Allâh and His Prophet ﷺ. When I disobey Him and His Prophet ﷺ, do not obey me."

By these words, Abu Bakr ﷺ set the rules for his government. He gave the people the right to dismiss him from power if he committed anything contrary to the principles of Islam.

The trouble Ahead

Some Arab tribes defied the state and thought of returning to paganism. Some of them announced that they were no longer obliged to be Muslims after the death of the Prophet ﷺ while others said that they were not ready to pay *Zakât*. Such movements were mainly at places in Arabia where Islam had not struck deep roots in the soil. Several impostors appeared claiming to have received revelation from Allâh.

Abu Bakr ﷺ, the new Caliph, had to face all these challenges and restore order. He was advised by some Companions especially 'Umar ﷺ, to be lenient. However, Abu Bakr ﷺ was well aware of the dangers that were threatening Islam and the Islamic State. He was decisive to put an end to such rebels. He prepared several armies to fight apostates. Finally, he controlled all of the rebels and brought them back to Islam.

The most important challenge was Musailimah *Al-Kadhab* (the Liar), in Najd. He gathered a huge army to fight the Muslims and for a while he was defeating any attempts to conquer his fortresses. However, he was finally conquered by an army led by Khalid bin Al-Waleed. So, the decisions of Abu Bakr ﷺ to fight the apostates and restore order and peace were very wise. He would have been satisfied to keep Al-Madinah and hence go back to the days when Islam first established itself in that town.

An expedition to be completed

Days before the death of the Prophet ﷺ, an army was mobilized to go north to fight the Romans who were preparing to attack the Muslims. However, this expedition was suspended because of the death of the Prophet ﷺ.

Abu Bakr ﷺ always carried out the commands of the Prophet

ﷺ. Therefore, he ordered Usamah bin Zaid ﷺ to lead the army as was originally commanded by the Prophet ﷺ. In spite of the fact that dangers were immense at home and although many Companions of the Prophet ﷺ preferred to abandon the expedition, Abu Bakr ﷺ was keen to carry out the orders of the Prophet ﷺ. He told those who objected to the expedition:

> "Who am I to stop the army that the Prophet ﷺ had ordered to proceed. Even if I was snatched by animals, I will send this army."

He gave his orders to the army to proceed and advised them:

> "Do not kill a child, an aged man or a woman. Do not cut trees or slay livestock except for your real needs. Do not bring harm to any monks. Now march forward in the Name of Allâh."

The expedition had placed fear in the hearts of Romans and Apostates alike. They saw that, in spite of the death of the Prophet ﷺ, the Islamic State was still strong enough to send such a big army.

Conquests under Abu Bakr's Rule

As Abu Bakr ﷺ was finished with the apostates in Arabia and brought them back to Islam, he directed his intentions to deter the Romans and Persians who already had bad intentions against the Islamic State. Both powers were creating trouble on the borders of the Islamic State. They had played a definite role in making other tribes revolt against the new government.

Conquest of Iraq

Under the leadership of Khalid bin Al-Waleed ﷺ, the famous Muslim commander, an army was mobilized to march to Iraq as a help to Muthana bin Harithah Al-Shaibani ﷺ. Arabs in the southern part of Iraq were badly treated by Persian landlords. The Muslims came to this land to save them from the oppression of the Persians.

Hurmuz, a Persian ruler, informed Chosroes, the Persian Emperor, about the advancing army. The Persians mobilized a huge army. Both armies engaged in a fierce battle. To the surprise of the Persians, their leader, Hurmuz, was killed on the spot. They immediately began fleeing the battlefield. The Muslim soldiers chased after them in a hot pursuit until they reached the Euphrates River.

Several other battles took place before the Muslims

conquered all of Iraq. They followed the orders of their Caliph to be merciful to the people of Iraq. This way of treatment made most people of Iraq and Madain embrace Islam.

Abu Bakr ﷺ felt that all such victories were due to Allâh's help and not to his or his soldiers' power. He thanked Allâh for his favour upon the Muslims, allowing them to gain control over one of the two major empires of the time.

Expedition to Syria

While the Muslims were fighting in Iraq, other armies were directed to the north to conquer the lands inhabited by Arabs in the southern parts of Syria and Palestine. The main objective behind such expeditions was self-defense. The Caliph wanted to strengthen his borders in order to prevent any attack from the side of the Romans. The Romans had already supported the apostates and were not happy to see the rebels fall one after the other.

Abu Bakr ﷺ mobilized a good army, divided into four parts and appointed four Commanders. He gave the army a farewell and advised the soldiers to always be just to people whom they conquer and to be sincere to their pledges. He was sure that the army would come back with victory.

Abu Bakr ﷺ remembered when the Prophet ﷺ prayed to Allâh at Badr for the small force of the Muslims to be victorious. Some of those men who fought at Badr joined this army to Syria.

Each faction of the army took a separate rout to Syria. All factions met at a place called Yarmouk. The leader, Abu 'Ubaidah bin Al-Jarrah ﷺ, saw how they were out-numbered by the Romans. He discussed the matter with his chiefs. They all agreed to inform Abu Bakr ﷺ of the conditions. Abu Bakr ﷺ ordered Khalid bin Al-Waleed ﷺ to leave the Iraqi front and speed up to Yarmouk. All commanders joined hands under the leadership of Khalid ﷺ. They fought a big battle and defeated the Romans once and for all.

The Virtues of Abu Bakr ﷺ

The Merciful

Abu Bakr ﷺ was known to be a very tender hearted man. He was very merciful to others even enemies. He showered love on all community members. He did not show favour to one over others. Surely he loved his children but the cause of Islam was dearer to him.

The Liberator

From the first day he accepted Islam, Abu Bakr ﷺ put all his resources under the service of the new religion. He bought the slaves who accepted Islam and freed them. He was charitable to all members of the society.

Full Dedication and Sacrifice

When the Prophet ﷺ instructed his Companions to prepare for the Tabuk expedition, he urged them to donate as much as they could out of their property. Abu Bakr ﷺ brought every things he had to the Prophet ﷺ. The Prophet ﷺ asked him how much he left for his family. He replied that he left them on the satisfaction of Allâh and His Prophet ﷺ.

No one among the Companions of the Prophet ﷺ excelled Abu Bakr ﷺ in terms of support of Islam. He usually gave the larger portion of his money for the cause of Islam.

Rule is a Responsibility

Assuming rule did not change the man. Immediately after taking over, he left his house to the market to sell some clothes for his living. 'Umar ﷺ saw him doing so. He immediately took him to the public treasurer and set him an annual salary to cover his needs.

It is reported that his wife asked him once to increase his share of sugar because she wanted to make some pudding. He told her that he could not do so. Therefore, she tried to save some quantity out of the monthly lot to fulfil her desire. When she had fulfilled that desire, she brought him the pudding. He immediately told the treasurer that his lot of sugar should be reduced because the quantity spared was not needed.

Collection of the Qur'ân

As a result of wars waged against the apostates, many prominent Companions of the Prophet ﷺ were killed. Among these people there were several persons who had memorized the Qur'ân. 'Umar ﷺ feared that the text of the Noble Qur'ân would be lost if such deaths continued. He asked Abu Bakr ﷺ to order for the collection of the Qur'ân. Abu Bakr ﷺ did not like to do something that the Prophet ﷺ did not himself do. However, 'Umar ﷺ convinced Abu Bakr ﷺ that such a job should be done; otherwise, the Qur'ân would be lost over time. Abu Bakr ﷺ accepted 'Umar's justifications and ordered Zaid bin Thabit ﷺ to collect the text of the Qur'ân.

Nomination of the Succeeding Caliph

Nearing his death, Abu Bakr ﷺ wanted to leave this worldly life free from obligations toward the nation. He discussed the issue of succession with many Companions. He suggested 'Umar ﷺ to be the successor Caliph and they all agreed that it was a good choice. Hence he wrote a testament in which he named 'Umar ﷺ as the next Caliph. In this very testament he advised the coming Caliph to care for the nation and to fear Allâh when deciding on any matter related to the State.

Before Leaving

Abu Bakr ﷺ felt that he was close to leaving this world. He called his daughter 'Âishah رضى الله عنها, the Prophet's wife. He asked her to calculate how much he had taken from the public treasury as post allowance. She told him that the total sum was six thousand dirhams. He ordered her to return the sum to the public treasury. Some reports say that he had left nothing for his children and relatives.

Joining the Prophet ﷺ in Eternal Life

Toward the end of his rule, Abu Bakr ﷺ was stricken by fever. He fell ill for several days before leaving this earthly abode. He had now fulfilled all his obligations. So, he longed to join the Prophet ﷺ in the hereafter. He passed away like any other human being.

On the bed of death, Abu Bakr ﷺ was seen several times weeping. He did not cry because of fear of death but because he might have neglected things that he was entrusted to do. After several days, Abu Bakr ﷺ passed away. The nation was very sad to lose the First Rightly Guided Caliph who fulfilled all of his obligations before Allâh and toward the nation of Islam. Abu Bakr ﷺ was buried beside the Prophet ﷺ in the room of 'Âishah رضى الله عنها.

May Allâh bestow his mercy on Abu Bakr ﷺ for the services he gave to Islam and the Muslims. He is still considered until today an example of dedication and sacrifice for Islam.

★★★

عـمـر بـن الخـطـاب رضي الله عنه

– ثاني الخلفاء الراشـــدين –

'Umar bin Al-Khattab رضي الله عنه

The Second Caliph of Islam

Umar accepts to Islam

Background

'Umar bin Al-Khattab belonged to a clan of high rank amongst the Quraish tribe. He was born forty years before the emigration of the Muslims to Al-Madinah in a house of dignity and honour. His father, Al-Khattab, was the chief of the Bani Makhzoum clan.

When 'Umar was a boy, his father treated him very harshly. He usually spent most of his time in the desert grazing camels for his father. However, when he became a young man, he began learning how to be a good merchant. He was also trained in wrestling and horsemanship until he became an example of strength and skill in both arts.

At that time, the Arabs were mostly illiterate. A few people knew how to read and write Arabic. 'Umar began learning how to read and write Arabic, which he mastered within a short period.

While still young, 'Umar traveled to many countries as a merchant and met many prominent people in both Syria and Iraq. He also acquired good knowledge of the affairs of the Roman and Persian Empires which were governing the world at that time.

'Umar was a well-known personality all over the Arabian

Peninsula. He was also feared by other chiefs because of his strength and position amongst the Quraish tribe.

When Muhammad ﷺ proclaimed the message of Islam, 'Umar took the side of the opposition. He was very hard on the few early Muslims. He used to beat his housemaid harshly because she accepted Islam. He did his best to make her and the other new Muslims abandon their faith. His relatives who accepted Islam kept their conversion to Islam secret for fear that he might torture them.

Intentions to kill the Prophet ﷺ

'Umar knew how steadfast the Muslims were to their faith. He used all means to make them go back to the worship of idols, but his efforts were all in vain. Therefore, he decided to kill the Prophet ﷺ himself in order to put an end to the message of Islam.

In a moment of rage, 'Umar took his sword and headed to the place where the Prophet ﷺ was teaching his followers the principles of Islam. On the way there, he met one of his tribesman named Na'eem bin 'Abdullah ﷺ, who had already accepted Islam but kept it secret. Na'eem ﷺ saw the signs of anger on 'Umar's face. He asked him where he was going. 'Umar angrily replied that he was going to kill Muhammad because he abused the idols of the Arabs. Na'eem ﷺ wanted 'Umar to change his direction. Therefore, he told him that it was better for him to settle his case with his sister and her husband before killing Muhammad ﷺ.

'Umar was astonished to learn that his sister, Fatimah, and her husband, Sa'eed, had accepted Islam. He changed his way and hurried to his sister's house. Upon arriving there, he stood at the door listening. To his surprise, he heard his sister, her husband and a third person reading the Qur'ân. He knocked at the door and waited for someone to open it. His sister immediately hid the papers they were reading and asked Khabbâb bin Al-Aratt ﷺ, the teacher, to hide. She opened the door and came face to face with 'Umar. He immediately asked her what they were reading. She denied reading anything. He slapped her on the face. Her nose began bleeding. Her husband tried to interfere but 'Umar pushed him back harshly. Fatimah decided that it was better to tell him the truth. She strongly said that she and her husband had accepted Islam and that they would not change their faith even if he killed them.

Signs of the Change

'Umar looked at his sister's face with her bleeding nose. His anger vanished and he felt sorry for what he had done. He calmly asked her to show him what they were reading. She gave him the papers and 'Umar began reading the Verses of the Qur'ân:

> "*Tâ-Hâ*. We have not sent down the Qur'ân to you (O Muhammad ﷺ) to cause distress. But only as a Reminder to those who fear (Allâh). A revelation from Him (Allâh) Who created the earth and high heavens." (20:1-4)

'Umar's face began changing and his heart softened. He felt a serenity that he had never felt before. Tears began rolling down his cheeks as a result of the impact of the nice words he was reading. He immediately asked his sister's husband to take him to the Prophet ﷺ. Upon hearing these words, Khabbab bin Al-Aratt ﷺ left his hiding place and told 'Umar that he had heard the Prophet ﷺ praying to Allâh to guide 'Umar to the way of Islam. He told 'Umar that the Prophet ﷺ and his Companions were in Dar Al-Arqam house.

Meeting the Prophet ﷺ

'Umar apologized for his rudeness toward his sister and her husband and left to the place where the Prophet ﷺ and his Companions gathered. He knocked at the door and waited for someone to open. A Companion of the Prophet ﷺ peeped through the cracks of the door and saw 'Umar with a sword at his side standing at the door. He told the Prophet ﷺ that it was 'Umar. The Companions of the Prophet ﷺ felt afraid because they knew how hard 'Umar was on the Muslims. The Prophet ﷺ asked the man to open the door. As 'Umar went in, the Prophet ﷺ threatened him that he feared that Allâh would punish him for his cruelty towards the Muslims. He then asked him about the reason for coming to him. 'Umar immediately said that he came to embrace Islam. The Muslims inside the room were very happy to hear these words from 'Umar.

'Umar declares His Conversion to Islam Publicly

Immediately after embracing Islam, 'Umar ﷺ went to the Ka'bah and announced before the chiefs of the Quraish that he had believed in Islam and the Prophet ﷺ and that he would challenge them till the end of his life. A fight ensued and the pagans attacked 'Umar ﷺ, but he bravely fought them all until an elderly man came and convinced the people to leave 'Umar ﷺ alone. From that day on, the Muslims felt strong and began worshipping Allâh openly. Historians confirmed that 'Umar ﷺ embraced Islam six years after the Prophet ﷺ was commissioned to proclaim the message of Islam. 'Abdullah bin Mas'ûd ﷺ said:

"After 'Umar accepted Islam we gained power and respect."

★★★

'Umar's Emigration to Al-Madinah

Oppression and Tyranny

The Muslims received all types of persecution at the hands of the chiefs of the Quraish. Many of them migrated to Abyssinia to escape the torture that the Quraish inflicted on them. 'Umar ﷺ and his fellow Muslims were striving to keep steadfast to their faith. Weak people and slaves who believed in the message of Islam were not able to withstand the oppression of the Quraish.

Attempts to Seek Protection

The Prophet ﷺ felt that there was no way out of such oppression but to emigrate to another land. He began calling tribes outside of Makkah to accept Islam and provide protection to him and his Companions. However, the chiefs of the Quraish were following his steps and defaming him before the visitors of Makkah.

The Prophet ﷺ decided to visit Tâ'if, a city near Makkah, to seek protection, but the chiefs of the Thaqeef tribe treated him very badly and rejected his call.

A group of people from a city called Yathrib (later known as Al-Madinah) visited Makkah. The Prophet ﷺ called them to accept Islam and provide protection for the Muslims. The group of people accepted the call and promised to come the next year with their chiefs to make an agreement with the Prophet ﷺ.

Islam spread quickly in Al-Madinah. Seventy men and a few women visited Makkah that year to hold a pledge of loyalty with the Prophet ﷺ. They promised to provide all means possible to protect the Prophet ﷺ and his followers in their city. It should be noted that emigration was an act ordained by Allâh through the Prophet ﷺ and not only an act to have protection against persecution and oppression of the Quraish.

'Umar ﷺ emigrates to Al-Madinah

'Umar ﷺ and twenty people of his clan emigrated to Al-Madinah in daylight. He challenged the chiefs of the Quraish to stop him but no one of them dared stand in his way.

Upon arriving in Al-Madinah, 'Umar ﷺ settled at a place called Quba' near Al-Madinah. He and his fellow Muslims received a warm welcome in Al-Madinah. The Prophet ﷺ and his close Companion Abu Bakr ﷺ followed them after a short time. The first thing the Prophet ﷺ did after settling in Al-Madinah was strengthening the ties of Islamic brotherhood between the emigrants (from Makkah) and supporters (inhabitants of Al-Madinah). 'Umar ﷺ was made the brother in Islam of 'Utban bin Malik ﷺ, the chief of Bani Saleem clan. 'Umar ﷺ joined his brothers in Islam in establishing firm foundations for the new state. He also joined hands with the other Muslims in building the first mosque of Islam. The Prophet ﷺ discussed with his Companions a way to call the Muslims to prayer. Some of them suggested ringing a bell at times of prayer, some suggested blowing a horn and others proposed to raise a flag. The Prophet ﷺ did not support any of these suggestions. He wanted to have something special for the Muslims.

'Umar ﷺ was very concerned about finding a way to call to prayer. That very night he had a dream. A man holding a bell came to him. 'Umar ﷺ asked him to give him the bell to use it to call the Muslims to prayer. However, the man told him that he had something better than the bell. He told him that it was better to call to prayer by using the *Adhân*. The next morning, 'Umar ﷺ hurried to the Prophet ﷺ to tell him about the dream he had. Surprisingly, another man had the same dream. He told the Prophet ﷺ about his dream before 'Umar ﷺ did. The Prophet ﷺ welcomed the idea and asked Bilal ﷺ to climb on top of the roof of the mosque to call the Muslims to prayer.

Challenges to Islam

Attempts to recover the Stolen Property

When 'Umar ﷺ and his fellow Muslims emigrated to Al-Madinah, they left behind all their property in Makkah, which the pagans took. The Muslims wanted to recover their property. A caravan led by Abu Sufyan was heading to Makkah back from Damascus loaded with all types of goods. The Prophet ﷺ instructed his Companions to capture the caravan. However, Abu Sufyan knew of the plan and changed his way. At the same time, he sent a man to the Quraish to warn them.

The Battle of Badr

The pagans gathered an army of about one thousand fighters and headed to Al-Madinah to save their caravan and to put an end to the threats of the Muslims. Although they were informed that the caravan had escaped from the Muslims, they insisted on fighting the Muslims and destroying their new state.

The Prophet ﷺ and his Companions received news of this huge army. They discussed how to face the challenge. They barely gathered an army of three hundred and thirteen fighters and marched to a place called Badr near Al-Madinah. 'Umar ﷺ prepared himself for the first battle against those who treated the Muslims with cruelty. He decided to show them that although the Muslims were weak, they could defeat the idolaters with the support of Allâh and strong Faith.

The battle started fiercely. 'Umar's main concern was to protect his Faith. During the battle, he came face to face with his uncle. He did not hesitate to kill his uncle because the latter came with the intention to destroy Islam. Although the number of the Muslim army was small compared to the number of their enemy, they defeated them. Seventy of the pagans were killed in the battle and the Muslims took another seventy soldiers as prisoners of war.

Revelation Supports 'Umar's Point of View

Upon returning to Al-Madinah, the Prophet ﷺ discussed with his Companions the issue of the prisoners of war. Abu Bakr ﷺ convinced the Prophet ﷺ that it would be better to take ransom money from them while 'Umar ﷺ insisted on killing them because they were the aggressors. However, the Prophet ﷺ took the side of Abu Bakr ﷺ. A while later, revelation came down supporting 'Umar's point of view that the prisoners of war should have been killed so that they could not fight against the Muslims again.

Other Challenges Against Islam

'Umar ﷺ continued his struggle for the sake of Islam. He did not miss any chance that would add to the strength of the newborn state of Islam. In the battle of Uhud, he and the other Muslims fought a hard battle. Although the Muslims lost the battle, 'Umar ﷺ and his fellow Muslims kept steadfast to their faith. Two years later, the pagans gathered a huge army and wanted to destroy the Islamic State. However, 'Umar ﷺ and the other Muslims dug a trench around Al-Madinah that stopped the pagans and prevented them from entering the city. After a siege for one month, the pagans withdrew in humiliation back to Makkah.

The Treaty

One year later, the Prophet ﷺ and his Companions wanted to visit Makkah to perform '*Umrah*. Although the Muslims wanted their journey to be peaceful, the pagans prevented them from entering Makkah. At a place called Al-Hudaibiyah, the Prophet ﷺ and his Companions negotiated with the Makkans to reach a peace agreement. The pagans insisted on putting a condition in the agreement stating that if anyone from the Muslims wished to join the pagans he should be given the freedom to do so, but if anyone from the pagans wished to join the Muslims, he should be sent back to the pagans by the Muslims. 'Umar ﷺ felt that this condition was humiliating to the Muslims. He was very angry and wanted the Prophet ﷺ to refuse such an unjust condition. The Prophet ﷺ told him that he was the Messenger of Allâh and that Allâh would support him. Later on, 'Umar ﷺ knew that the agreement was in the good interest of the Muslims. It gave the Muslims a chance to stop fighting with the main power in the Arabian Peninsula and call other tribes of Arabia to Islam. Several tribes accepted Islam and joined in building the Islamic State.

Conquest of Makkah

The Quraish failed to respect their agreement with the Muslims. They broke their promise and killed some of the Muslims' allies. The Prophet ﷺ and the Muslims were now determined to put an end to idolatry in Makkah. 'Umar ﷺ joined the army of ten thousand Muslims who marched to Makkah and conquered the city. 'Umar ﷺ wanted to revenge himself against the pagans who oppressed the Muslims. However, the Prophet ﷺ taught him that a triumphant believer should always be forgiving. The Prophet ﷺ told the people of Makkah that they were free. In reaction to this merciful attitude by the Prophet ﷺ, all the people of Makkah accepted Islam. 'Umar ﷺ was beside the Prophet ﷺ when the women of Makkah came to embrace Islam. The Prophet ﷺ asked 'Umar ﷺ to be his deputy in witnessing the acceptance of Islam by the women.

The Prophet ﷺ Passes Away

As Makkah had now become a Muslim land, the Prophet ﷺ told his Companions that he wished to perform pilgrimage. 'Umar ﷺ, along with one hundred thousand Muslims, accompanied the Prophet ﷺ to Makkah to perform pilgrimage. Upon completing the pilgrimage rites, the Prophet ﷺ addressed his Companions about the everlasting principles of Islam. In his speech, he implied that he would pass away soon. 'Umar ﷺ felt very sad to hear these words from the Prophet ﷺ. Upon returning to Al-Madinah, the Prophet ﷺ fell ill. After a short period, he passed away. When 'Umar ﷺ was told that the Prophet ﷺ had passed away, he did not believe the news. He unsheathed his sword and threatened to kill anyone who might say that the Prophet ﷺ had died. He loved the Prophet ﷺ dearly and wanted him to remain alive among the Muslims to direct them if they did something wrong. He was calmed down and convinced by Abu Bakr ﷺ that the Prophet ﷺ had died indeed.

The Selection of the Caliph

While 'Umar ﷺ and other close Companions of the Prophet ﷺ were busy with the Prophet's funeral, a group from the *Ansâr* (supporters) gathered at a place called As-Saqifah to select a Caliph (ruler) from among them. Someone told 'Umar of this meeting and he along with Abu Bakr and Abu 'Ubaidah bin Al-Jarrah & left the funeral and went to As-Saqifah. 'Umar convinced the supporters that Abu Bakr should be the Caliph. They all accepted his selection of Abu Bakr and pledged obedience.

'Umar ﷺ, the Caliph

Before passing away, Abu Bakr ﷺ consulted the senior Companions of the Prophet ﷺ about the best man to succeed him. They all agreed that 'Umar ﷺ would be the best Caliph.

As 'Umar ﷺ took over, he started organizing the affairs of the state relying on the teachings of the Qur'ân and the Prophet's sayings.

Achievements of 'Umar ﷺ during his Rule

With the spread of the Islamic State over Iraq, Syria and Egypt, 'Umar ﷺ found it necessary to establish firm regulations under which the rulers of different regions should deal with their subjects. He sent letters containing rules of government to the governors. Not only this, but he also made visits to some parts of the Islamic Empire to ensure that the governors he appointed were treating people justly.

'Umar ﷺ also established the public treasury. The money brought to the treasury was equally distributed among the Muslims. Records of soldiers were made so as to pay them their wages wherever they were. The army was organized in a way very similar to the modern armies. Every seven soldiers were headed by a supervisor who was responsible for their wages and benefits. 'Umar ﷺ also appointed judges to solve problems among the Muslims. He himself was summoned before the judge on at least two occasions. He recruited watchmen to guard the streets during the night and established a system of controls on markets to prevent any ways of deceit.

Public facilities and construction of cities were also part of his interests. He ordered the building of Kufah, Basrah and Mausil in Iraq and Fustat and Jiza in Egypt. He himself prepared the layouts of these cities. Spaces for streets and alleys were determined by 'Umar ﷺ himself. Rivers and canals were also dug to provide water to populated areas all over the Islamic State. Engineers and craftsmen from all parts of the state were mobilized to pave roads in order for caravans to travel with ease throughout the vast state.

'Umar ﷺ found that it was essential for all Muslims to learn how to read the Noble Qur'ân. Therefore, he sent teachers to all parts of the state to teach people how to recite the Noble Qur'ân. He also set prizes for those who memorized the Qur'ân within a short period. Scholars among the Prophet's Companions were directed to teach people the interpretation of the Qur'ân and the principles of the *Sharî'ah* (Islamic law). Bedouins were given much attention. Teaching of their children was established as a mandatory law. *Muftis* (legal advisors) were also appointed to give answers to legal questions.

'Umar ﷺ paid much attention to construction of mosques. He gave orders to expand the Sacred Mosque in Makkah as its space was not sufficient to accommodate visitors. He also supervised expansion of the Prophet's Mosque in Al-Madinah for the same reasons. He wrote to all governors ordering them to build mosques in cities and villages. It is reported that the number of mosques built during 'Umar's rule was more than three thousand.

The Arabs had no certain event to set the calendar. 'Umar ﷺ was receiving letters from governors that were not dated with a year. He discussed the matter with his advisors. They all agreed to his point of view that the year of the *Hijrah* (emigration to Al-Madinah) should be the first year of the Islamic calendar.

As most people of the conquered lands, especially Iraq, Syria and Egypt were farmers, 'Umar ﷺ ordered for their lands to be kept under their own control because they were familiar with the methods of cultivation. In addition, he provided farmers with all means necessary to increase and diversify their crops.

In addition to the records and bureaus, 'Umar, ﷺ established for the military and civilians of the Islamic society, he ordered construction of barracks for the army at the borders of the Islamic State. This allowed the soldiers to use these as places of residence away from their homeland. He also set rules of service for soldiers. No soldier should keep away from his family more than four months so as to keep in touch with his family. Mail from soldiers was sometimes distributed by 'Umar ﷺ himself.

As the road from Al-Madinah to Makkah was hard for pilgrims and visitors, 'Umar ﷺ gave orders to pave the road, establish shaded rest places and dig wells to provide water to caravans.

Care for the Nation

The services rendered during the rule of 'Umar ﷺ did not

cover Muslims only but were extended to all the subjects of the state. Old non-Muslim men and women were given maintenance pay. Subsidies were also given to farmers and craftsmen to help them continue their businesses. Every poor member of the nation was receiving a welfare stipend including newborns.

Honorable Treatment of Conquered People

Palestine was mainly inhabited by Christians. When the Muslims conquered it, the inhabitants of *Al-Quds* (Jerusalem) agreed to surrender the city peacefully to the Muslim army. They knew that 'Umar ﷺ was a just ruler. Therefore, they wanted him to sign the agreement himself. 'Umar ﷺ left Al-Madinah and visited *Al-Quds* to make the agreement. It was reported that he was not accompanied by any guards except his servant. He concluded an agreement with the inhabitants of the city, which guaranteed them all their financial and religious rights. As a result, most of the city inhabitants accepted Islam.

★★★

Conquests under 'Umar's Rule

Conquests in Iraq and Iran

During Abu Bakr's rule, the Muslim armies spread east and north for the propagation of Islam. Before conquering the Persians and the Romans, Abu Bakr ﷺ died and left the trust to 'Umar ﷺ. 'Umar ﷺ continued the efforts started by Abu Bakr ﷺ to conquer the two major nations of the time.

'Umar ﷺ selected Sa'd bin Abi Waqqâs ﷺ to conquer Persia. An army of thirty thousand soldiers was gathered to fulfil the mission. Before leaving Al-Madinah, 'Umar ﷺ advised Sa'd ﷺ saying:

> "Sa'd, I order you to fight the Persians. Listen to me and hold fast to my words. You are going to face a very hard obstacle that you cannot overcome unless you observe truth and goodness. You should know that every battle should be prepared for by having good equipment. Let your equipment be patience. Do not be deceived by saying to yourself 'I am the Prophet's uncle' for there is no kinship dearer to Allâh than obedience to His teachings."

Sa'd ﷺ led the army to a place called Al-Qâ-disiyah in Iraq. There he saw the Persians deploying their army under the leadership of Rustam.

'Umar wrote a letter to Sa'd saying:

"I order you and your soldiers to fear Allâh at all times, for fearing Allâh is the best weapon you have against your enemy. I order you and your soldiers to guard against evil deeds as much as you guard against your enemy. Evil deeds are more dangerous to your army than your enemy is. You will win because your enemy is a disbeliever. Ask Allâh to help you overcome your desires as much as you ask Him to help you overcome your enemy. Do not cause Muslims to march when they are tired and keep them ready with full strength to meet the enemy. Take rest one day every week to keep your army fully ready. Do not come near any village inhabited by our protected peaceful allies and do not allow anyone of your army to enter any village unless you are sure he will act properly. Lookout scouting is the best way to know the power of your enemy. Therefore, give such a mission to whom you most trust and provide them with the best horses."

Sa'd sent messengers to Yazdajurd, the Persian King, calling him to embrace Islam, to pay tribute or if he rejected both options, to fight.

The first delegation called the King to accept Islam. Instead of accepting this kind call, the King began blaming the Muslims for coming to his land and threatened to destroy their religion. The King showed the delegation much humiliation and anger. He asked his soldiers to fill sacks of soil and force the members of the delegation to carry them on their backs till they left the city. He told them that he would send Rustam to bury their leader and the Muslim army in Al-Qâdisiyah trench.

Rustam foresaw signs of defeat in the acts of the King. Therefore, he asked Sa'd ﷺ to send him another messenger to negotiate. Al-Mugheerah bin Shu'bah ﷺ came to Rustam. As soon as he arrived, Rustam started negotiating with him in a very gentle manner and asked him to tell Sa'd ﷺ that it was better for the Muslims to leave their homeland. Al-Mugheerah ﷺ told Rustam that it was their mission to spread the light of Islam. He explained to him the principles of Islam.

Rustam felt the just teachings of Islam and asked the messenger to give him time to discuss with the heads of the nation. Rustam told his people that it was better for them to accept Islam, but they refused.

Sa'd ﷺ sent the third messenger, Reb'iy bin 'Amir ﷺ to Rustam. Before his arrival to the place of the Persian army, the Persians wanted to show him how rich and powerful they were. The whole palace was furnished with gold and silver. Reb'iy ﷺ came inside with his humble dress on his horse until he stepped on the carpets and spoilt them with his spear. He jumped down from the back of his horse and sat beside Rustam. He was not amazed by the vanity they wanted to show him. The negotiations did not yield any fruits.

More messengers were sent but all attempts to reach a solution came to nothing. At last, Rustam told Sa'd ﷺ that he would give the Muslims a bitter defeat if they insisted on fighting.

The Persians prepared about one hundred thousand fully armed soldiers supported by elephants and other heavy combat equipment. The Muslims on the opposite side gathered their humble arms to fight against this huge army.

The timing of operations was initiated by the words *Allâhu Akbar* (Allâh is the Greatest). The Muslim army faced a sudden shock. Their horses did not move forward for fear of the advancing elephants that the Persians put in the first line. However, some Muslim fighters began shooting the elephants. They forced the elephants to retreat in terror and throw off their riders. The whole day of fighting did not change the positions of either army. The second day a new round of fighting started. The Muslims received support by an army led by Hashim bin 'Utbah coming from Damascus. However, victory was achieved by neither army.

On the third day, the Persians prepared for another surprise. They put some huge elephants ahead of the army and attacked the Muslim army. The attack was almost successful. However, some Muslim commandos led by Al-Qa'qâ' bin 'Amr attacked the elephants and forced them to turn back through the advancing army. The Muslims then opened huge gaps through the Persian army.

The battle continued and the Muslims were sacrificing their souls to raise the Islamic banner high. The fighting went on all the night. When the sun rose, it was clear that the Muslims had the upper hand.

Rustam tried to escape but he was finally killed. The succeeding commander, Galinos, tried to save the defeated army by crossing to the other bank of the Tigris River. Instead, more than thirty thousand of his soldiers drowned in the river.

Sa'd ordered his army to follow the fleeing army until he

was sure that victory was fully achieved. The battle was over and Sa'd ﷺ immediately sent a messenger to 'Umar ﷺ informing him of the victory they achieved and asking for further orders. 'Umar ﷺ ordered Sa'd ﷺ to continue his march to Mada'in, the Persian capital. The Muslims marched forth but did not meet any resistance on the way to the capital.

The Muslim army led by Sa'd ﷺ did not have any boats to cross the Tigris River. Sa'd ﷺ ordered his soldiers to cross the river on horse backs. Not one of them was stopped by the torrent of the river. The Persian soldiers on the opposite bank of the river thought that they were fighting against genies. Salman Al-Farisi ﷺ (a great Companion of the Prophet, ﷺ originally from Persia) foresaw the heavenly help given to Muslims. He shouted:

> " I swear by Allâh, those who had overcome the mainland would surely overcome the sea."

The Muslim army surprised the Persian army who fled the city. Mada'in was conquered and the Persian Empire was defeated forever.

Conquests in Syria and Palestine

Abu Bakr ﷺ appointed Khalid bin Al-Waleed ﷺ as Commander General of the Muslim army. He was fighting the Persians in Iraq but was directed by Abu Bakr ﷺ to support the army led by Abu 'Ubaidah bin Al-Jarrah ﷺ who was directed to conquer the Romans.

The Romans gathered an army of two hundred thousand soldiers while the Muslim army numbered about thirty thousand fighters. Both armies met near a village called Al-Yarmouk. Khalid ﷺ carefully studied the conditions and set up plans to fight the coming battle.

Before the start of the battle, the Roman commander sought to meet Khalid ﷺ. He agreed to meet with him. The Roman commander addressed Khalid ﷺ saying:

> "It has been brought to our knowledge that poverty was the only reason that brought you out of your land to here. If you wish, I will give each one of you ten dinars, clothes and food on the condition that you go back to your land. I will even reward you with equal portions next year."

Khalid ﷺ angrily responded to such a belittling address saying:

> "It is not poverty that brought us here; rather, it is that we only wish to drink your blood. We have been told it is most tasty."

Khalid ﷺ returned to his troops. He studied the battlefield and decided to divide his army into battalions along the line of combat to face the huge number of the Roman army.

Soon the rattle of swords and cries of *Allâhu Akbar* (Allâh is the Greatest) filled the air and heads fell under horses' hooves. Both armies fought all day long. They became very tired and retreated to their original positions. On the next day, Khalid ﷺ and his soldiers attacked the heart of the Roman army and divided their lines. The Romans, on the other side, began retreating and fleeing in all directions. They suffered a huge loss and left the battlefield in humiliation.

While the battle was hot, a messenger from Al-Madinah arrived with news that Abu Bakr ﷺ had died, that 'Umar ﷺ was selected as the Caliph and that Khalid ﷺ was to be replaced by

Abu 'Ubaidah bin Al-Jarrah ﷺ. Abu 'Ubaidah ﷺ kept the news secret until the Romans were finally defeated. He met Khalid ﷺ and informed him of the news. Khalid ﷺ willingly handed over the command to Abu 'Umbaidah ﷺ and continued as an ordinary soldier under Abu 'Ubaidah's command. Abu 'Ubaidah ﷺ continued his march. He conquered Damascus and its surrounding areas. The Roman Emperor left his place of rule in Hims and paid Syria an eternal farewell. Following this great victory, Abu 'Ubaidah ﷺ led his army to *Al-Quds* (Jerusalem). The chiefs of the city surrendered the city peacefully. They asked the leader to make an agreement which, upon their request, was to be signed by 'Umar ﷺ himself.

Conquest of Egypt

'Umar ﷺ continued his efforts of spreading the light of Islam. He prepared an army under the leadership of 'Amr bin Al-'Aas ﷺ to conquer Egypt. Within a short period of time, 'Amr ﷺ defeated the Romans and saved the Egyptians from their injustices. He built a strong Muslim state in Egypt under the guidance of 'Umar bin Al-Khattab ﷺ.

Virtues of 'Umar bin Al-Khattab

Humility

'Umar was known as a very humble man. He used to help the orphans and widows to manage their lives. Once he was walking with his servant through the streets of Al-Madinah during the night. He heard some children crying. He found that a poor woman was trying to calm down her hungry children by putting an empty pot on the fire to show them that she was making them some food. 'Umar went back to the warehouse and took some flour and meat, carried them on his back and returned to the woman. He began cooking for the children and giving them food. He left them very happy. It was reported that he also visited an old woman every night to care for her and satisfy her needs.

Justice

A Jew complained against 'Umar to the judge, 'Ali bin Abi Tâlib. 'Ali summoned 'Umar and the Jew before him to settle the case. 'Umar was very happy that 'Ali made him stand beside the Jew in the court and did not distinguish him over the Jew.

The son of 'Amr bin Al-'Aas, the governor of Egypt, entered a race on horses with an Egyptian. The Egyptian won the race. 'Amr's son got angry and whipped the Egyptian because he won the race. The Egyptian came to 'Umar complaining against 'Amr's son. 'Umar sent for 'Amr and his son to appear before him. Upon appearing before him, 'Umar asked the Egyptian to whip 'Amr's son as he had whipped him. 'Umar addressed 'Amr saying:

"Since when do you started to enslave people when they were born free."

Fear of Allâh

'Umar was always expressing his fear of meeting Allâh on the Day of Judgment with any sins. Sometimes, he was heard saying:

"I would be satisfied if Allâh pardons me in the Hereafter."

He ordered all his governors all over the Islamic State to be kind even to animals for fear that he might be responsible for any injustice they might cause to people. He said:

"I fear that if a mule stumbles in Iraq, I will be questioned as to why I did not pave the way for it."

Tears drew two black lines on his cheeks for fear that he might be punished by Allâh. Although he was told by the Prophet that he would dwell in Paradise, he would pray most of the night in order to be acceptable to Allâh.

Sound Judgment

Some judgments given by 'Umar have become religious rules. One case was when he asked the Prophet to order women to wear *Hijab* (Islamic dress). Allâh supported his opinion and Qur'ânic revelation came down ordaining the same. The Prophet said:

"If there were divinely inspired men in my nation, it would be 'Umar."

The End

As usual, 'Umar ﷺ made pilgrimage to Makkah in the beginning of the eleventh year of his rule. The Islamic state had by now spread over Syria, Egypt, Persia and some parts of the Byzantine Empire. This quick spread of Islam was hated and envied by all enemies of Islam. They would try now and then to thwart Islam but in vain.

'Umar ﷺ used to go to *Fajr* (Dawn) prayer unattended by any guards. He left his house to the mosque in the dark, ordered for the prayer to be performed and stood in front of the lines as leader of the prayer. A Persian named Fairuz had planned to kill the Caliph. He decided to do his crime during the prayer. As 'Umar ﷺ started the prayer, Fairuz stepped forward and stabbed him several times in his side with a dagger. He also killed other Muslims who were trying to get hold of him. 'Umar ﷺ retreated to the first row and ordered his son to complete the prayer as the leader. The persons behind him saw this criminal act by the Persian. They tried to catch him but he killed himself.

'Umar ﷺ was taken home. He asked who could be the man who stabbed him. They told him that it was Fairuz. 'Umar ﷺ thanked Allâh that the killer was not a Muslim. He was well aware that the enemies of Islam would not allow its message to be spread in peace.

Before dying, he selected six men and ordered that one among them to be selected as the Caliph. He also asked the permission of Aishah رضي الله عنها (the Prophet's wife) to be buried beside the Prophet ﷺ. She agreed although she wanted to keep the place for herself. Three days later 'Umar ﷺ passed away.

'Umar ﷺ was buried beside the Prophet ﷺ and Abu Bakr ﷺ. He lied there in peace to meet with the Prophet ﷺ and his Companions on the Day of Judgment fully satisfied that he did his best to spread the Word of Allâh.

May Allâh bestow his mercy on 'Umar ﷺ, the best example of justice, for the great services he rendered to Islam and the Muslims.

We should all remember 'Umar ﷺ with great gratitude. Had it not been for the help of Allâh and the efforts exerted by 'Umar ﷺ, the Islamic State would not have spread over the world.

عثمان بن عفان رضي الله عنه

— ثالث الخلفاء الراشدين —

Uthman bin Affam رضي الله عنه

The Third Caliph of Islam

The Son of the Merchent

Background

Uthman was born to a rich family. His father was a well-known merchant. His trade went as far as Damascus and many other parts of the Arabian Peninsula. His wealthy father provided him with everything to help him lead an easy and happy life. Uthman was brought up the way other children born to high class families were raised. He enjoyed all the things that people from high-class backgrounds enjoyed. Uthman, however, had a personality that could see beyond the riches of this short life. He had good morals. Some of his special characteristics were that he was a very bashful, truthful and generous person. Uthman was still young when his father passed away during a journey to Damascus. This left him in charge of his father's business that he ran very efficiently.

Like Father like Son

Like his father, Uthman became a well-known trader. However, unlike any other merchant, Uthman spent most of his profits on feeding the poor and the needy. It was because of this characteristic that the people respected him and loved him very much. He would also give his wealth away to the public welfare. He was doing his best to draw a smile on miserable faces. No one other than Abu Bakr ﷺ could excel Uthman in respect of charity and love for the poor and the needy. On many occasions, he spent the major part of his money to equip an army or to provide a facility for Muslims.

The Light of Islam

Uthman was most of the time traveling either to Damascus or Yemen. During his long journeys he was dealing with people from different nations. He heard many things different from his beliefs and established doctrines. Christians and Jews, known those days to be the "People of the Book", changed many ideas he had about idols and the life of Arabs.

Signs of Change

After a long journey to Damascus, Uthman returned to Makkah to find it amid turmoil. All the people were speaking of Muhammad bin Abdullah. The man had presented himself to them as the Prophet of Islam and brought them new ideas and precepts that they had never heard of. Uthman knew Muhammad ﷺ very well and was well aware of his very good personality and excellent morals. So, he did not oppose the new religion like other chiefs of the Quraish tribe did. On many occasions during his travels, Uthman heard the Jewish and Christian scholars talk about the coming of a new Prophet in the land of Arabia. Uthman was always thinking about the Prophet ﷺ who would change the life of the Arabs and take them out of the gloomy life that they were leading, into a life of knowledge and guidance. After some thought, Uthman made his way straight to his friend Abu Bakr's house to find out more about the new religion. Abu Bakr was very close to the Prophet and he had already accepted Islam. Abu Bakr told Uthman that Islam called people to worship Allâh Alone, and to give up the worship of false idols. He asked Uthman with a firm tone:

> "What are these idols that your people worship? Are they not just stones that can neither hear nor see, and can neither bring good nor harm to anyone?"

Abu Bakr urged Uthman to accept Islam, the true religion of Allâh, and to give up the false worship of idols. Uthman knew in his heart that Islam was the true religion of Allâh and so he accepted the invitation and immediately embraced Islam. He was one of the few early Muslims. Uthman was a young man full of spirit. He went to Muhammad and declared his submission to the new religion.

Suffering for his Belief

Muslims were facing huge hardships at the hands of pagans. Like any person embracing Islam, Uthman was also exposed to oppression. His uncle, Al-Hakam bin Abi Al-'Aas, was very angry that Uthman had abandoned the religion of his forefathers. He tied him up and told him that he would not let him free until he would go back to his old religion. Uthman suffered for several days, but he stayed steadfast to his beliefs. He told his uncle very clearly that he would never abandon Islam. Eventually, when his uncle realized that Uthman would never submit to his will, he set him free. Since the day Uthman accepted Islam, he always kept close to the Prophet supporting the new religion and defending the new light of guidance. He did everything he could to defend Islam and never gave in to the Quraish's torture and oppression. Muslims were subjected to all types of torture. Some of them were even killed for embracing Islam. Uthman ﷺ was one of the first people to migrate to Abyssinia, followed by the other Muslims who were being harassed by the Quraish to abandon Islam.

Migration to Abyssinia

Uthman ﷺ was married to the Prophet's daughter named Ruqayah رضي الله عنها. Uthman ﷺ took his wife and left to Abyssinia to escape the oppression of the Quraish. Upon arrival there, Uthman ﷺ and the other Muslims tried to live in peace and worship Allâh as they wished.

The Quraish chiefs were angry to see the Muslims leave Makkah and escape their control and tyranny. They attempted all ways to prevent the Muslims from leaving Makkah, but all their efforts were unsuccessful. The Quraish chiefs discussed ways to have the Muslims brought back to Makkah. Some of them were trading with Abyssinia. They knew the Emperor (An-Najashi) personally. They thought that sending some presents to the Emperor would help them get their slaves and relatives.

Abu Sufyan and others suggested that they should send 'Amr bin Al-'Aas to An-Najashi to get the Muslims back to Makkah. 'Amr bin Al-'Aas knew An-Najashi very well. They were friends. The Quraish collected nice gifts to be presented to the Emperor and urged 'Amr bin Al-'Aas to use his friendship with the Emperor to realize their objectives.

'Amr bin Al-'Aas arrived in Abyssinia and sought to meet the Emperor. He set a plot to make the Emperor expel the migrants from his land or even surrender them to the Quraish. Upon meeting the Emperor, 'Amr presented to him the gifts sent by the Quraish which the Emperor liked very much. The Emperor asked 'Amr if he could offer him any help.

'Amr took the chance to ask the Emperor to question the migrants who sought protection in his land. He said that they had left the religion of their people and followed a strange religion that was neither idol worshipping nor Christianity. The Emperor ordered the migrants to come to his court. He asked their leader, Ja'far bin Abi Tâlib ﷺ about the allegations made against them. Ja'far advanced to the middle of the court and said:

> "We were people of bad morals and faith. We worshipped idols of stone. We treated our neighbours in an evil way. We lived as such until a man from among us declared that he was ordered by Allâh to take us out of this darkness of morals and thought. We believed in him but our people did not leave us alone. They oppressed us, tortured us and left us no chance to worship Allâh as we wished. We, therefore, resorted to your land for we knew you were just and merciful."

The envoy of the Quraish felt that the response made by Ja'far ﷺ impressed the Emperor. He wanted to make another plot. He told the Emperor that the Muslims said bad things about Jesus Christ. The Emperor asked Ja'far ﷺ about their views of Jesus Christ. Ja'far ﷺ began reciting some Verses of *Surat Maryam*. He saw tears going down the cheeks of the Emperor and his court men. When he finished reciting, the Noble Qur'ân, the Emperor confirmed that the words recited by Ja'far ﷺ were the same ones preached by Jesus Christ. He dismissed 'Amr bin Al-'Aas and gave him back his presents. He told the migrants that they were free to live in his land and that no one would dare cause them any harm. So, Uthman ﷺ and the other migrants were very happy to have the Emperor on their side. They lived in peace in Abyssinia until they all emigrated to Al-Madinah.

Uthman ﷺ in Al-Madinah

As days went by, Islam was gaining more and more power and the number of Muslims was increasing. However, life in Makkah was becoming more and more difficult for Muslims as the Quraish were subjecting them to all kinds of oppression and torture.

New Plots Against the Muslims

Muslims who had migrated to Abyssinia received news that the Prophet ﷺ and the Quraish reached an agreement, and life in Makkah was better. Some of them left Abyssinia back to Makkah. However, they found that the information they had received was false. When they came back to Makkah they found that the situation was much worse than before. Some of them were caught by the pagans and were treated with cruelty.

Hunger and Deprivation

The Quraish decided to impose a boycott on the Muslims and Bani Hashim, the clan of the Prophet ﷺ. They cut all social, economic and familial relations with Muslims. They even isolated them in a valley to deprive them of any help from outside. Uthman ﷺ was among the Muslims isolated by the Quraish, but he did his best to ease the distress. He ordered his agents to buy food and bring it secretly to the Muslims. For three long years the Muslims suffered a lot from hunger.

Emigration to Al-Madinah

Out of His great mercy, Allâh wanted to help the Muslims. Some people came to visit the Ka'bah from Al-Madinah, which at that time was known as Yathrib. These people accepted Islam and promised to help and support the Muslims. The Prophet ﷺ wanted to save the lives and faith of his Companions, so he asked them to emigrate to Al-Madinah, where they would be protected from the evil plots of the Quraish. Uthman رضي الله عنه married the Prophet's daughter Ruqayah, who was divorced by 'Utba bin Abi Lahab. Abu Lahab was the Prophet's uncle. He was a bitter enemy of Islam. He wanted to threaten the Prophet ﷺ, so he asked his son 'Utba to divorce Ruqayah. Uthman رضي الله عنه asked to marry her and the Prophet ﷺ agreed to give her in marriage to his Companion. Both Uthman and Ruqayah رضي الله عنهما, along with the other Muslims migrated to Al-Madinah. They were both known to be the best husband and wife. When they got to Al-Madinah, they built a small house for themselves and lived together in peace. Many of the Companions of the Prophet ﷺ spent their money helping the Muslims, but the way of Uthman رضي الله عنه spending his money was very well known.

Spending Money for Allâh's Sake

Muslims were very poor in Al-Madinah. They had left all their property and flocks in Makkah. Their supporters in Al-Madinah shared with them all their resources. A Jew owned a well from which he sold water to the inhabitants of Al-Madinah at high prices. The inhabitants complained to the Prophet ﷺ about the high prices that the Jew was charging. When Uthman رضي الله عنه heard their complaint, he felt very sorry for the Muslims. So, he decided to do something to solve the problem. He immediately went to the Jew and offered him a high price for the well. The Jew, however, refused to sell the whole well and offered to sell half the well to Uthman ﷺ. The supply of water was divided between the two parties on a daily basis. Uthman ﷺ would use the well one day and the Jew would use it the next day. Uthman ﷺ asked the Muslims to take enough water for two days. So, when it was the Jew's day to sell water, no one was going to him to buy water. At last the Jew sold the second half of the well to Uthman ﷺ.

More Challenges

During the second year after the Muslims had emigrated to Al-Madinah, the Makkans gathered a huge army and headed towards Al-Madinah to put an end to Islam. When the Muslims heard of the army coming to destroy their religion, they too gathered an army of three hundred men. Both armies met at Badr, a place near Al-Madinah. Uthman ﷺ was not able to take part in this battle of Islam against the disbelievers because his wife Ruqayah رضي الله عنها was ill. The Prophet ﷺ asked him to stay behind and care for her. So, Uthman ﷺ stayed behind and looked after his ill wife. However, Ruqayah رضي الله عنها died a few days later.

The Man with *Dhun Nurain* (Two Lights)

Uthman ﷺ was very saddened by the death of Ruqayah رضي الله عنها. 'Umar bin Al-Khattab ﷺ asked Uthman ﷺ to marry his daughter Hafsah رضي الله عنها. Uthman ﷺ did not accept 'Umar's offer because he knew that the Prophet ﷺ wished to marry her. After a while, the Prophet ﷺ asked Uthman ﷺ to marry his second daughter Umm Kulthum رضي الله عنها who was also divorced by the second son of Abu Lahab. Uthman ﷺ accepted the Prophet's offer and the couple lived very happily together. Since that day, Uthman ﷺ was named as the man with two lights, meaning the two daughters of the Prophet ﷺ.

Defiant and Brave

In the sixth year after emigration to Al-Madinah, the Prophet ﷺ decided to perform pilgrimage. With one thousand four hundred Muslims in pilgrims' dress, Uthman ﷺ left to Makkah to perform pilgrimage. On the way, the Muslims learnt that the Quraish would not let them enter the city. At last, the Muslims reached a place called Hudaibiyah. They camped there. The Prophet ﷺ sent a messenger to the Makkans to convince them that the Muslims only wanted to perform the pilgrimage and had not the slightest intent to fight. However, the messenger was treated badly and returned without any success. The Prophet ﷺ then wanted to send someone who was highly respected by the Quraish. Uthman ﷺ was selected because of his kinship with the powerful Ummayad family. The Makkans, however, detained him for three days and news reached the Muslim camp that he had been killed. Without exception, all the one thousand four hundred Muslims gave a pledge that they would stand or fall together to avenge Uthman's murder. Such a pledge pleased Allâh and the Prophet ﷺ, soon it was known that the news of Uthman's murder was false.

The Unique Example of Sacrifice

During the time of the Prophet ﷺ, the Muslims had so much love for Islam that they would race one another in doing good deeds and making sacrifices for the religion of Allâh. However, none of them could excel Uthman ؓ except Abu Bakr ؓ. Uthman ؓ was a true and generous believer. He was so keen to please Allâh that he would sometimes sacrifice all his trade and property for the support of Islam. Uthman ؓ was so generous that he would give out of his money to all those around him.

As soon as the Prophet ﷺ entered Al-Madinah, he built a small mosque. This mosque was not like any other mosque. It was a place where the Muslims could gather for prayer, prepare for *Jihâd* (fighting disbelievers) and discuss the affairs of the Muslim community. As more and more people accepted Islam, the mosque became too small for the Muslims. The Prophet ﷺ was looking for someone to help expand the mosque. As soon as Uthman ؓ knew of this, he immediately went to the owner of the house beside the Mosque. He asked him to sell the house to him. The owner of the house asked for a high price. Uthman ؓ paid the price. He went to the Prophet ﷺ and told him that he would like to give the house to expand the Mosque. The Prophet ﷺ accepted the offer and was very pleased with Uthman ؓ.

In the ninth year after Hijrah, the Prophet ﷺ received news that the Romans were plotting to disrupt the Islamic State. The Romans wished to destroy the new emerging Islamic State. The Prophet ﷺ wanted to show the Romans that they were not so weak as to be taken easily. The Muslims suffered that particular year of reduced crops. The summer was very hot and resources were limited. Most of the Muslims were poor. They did not have enough resources to meet such a powerful army. The Prophet ﷺ, however, urged his Companions to prepare for the battle, which seemed an impossible task in the middle of the hot summer. The Muslims began preparing for the battle. The rich Companions of the Prophet ﷺ tried their best to equip the army. Women, on the other hand, began collecting their scarce jewelry to help the Muslims prepare for this battle.

Hundreds of soldiers were ready to go to the battlefield, but they were short of horses, camels and even swords and spears. The Prophet ﷺ urged his Companions to donate as much as they could for the army. He told them that it was a matter of life or death for the new Islamic State. He made a loud and clear announcement:

"Anyone who provides outfits for the soldiers will have all his sins forgiven by Allâh."

As soon as Uthman ﷺ heard these words, he immediately responded to the call and provided all that the army might need. As history books tell:

"Uthman ﷺ provided for Tabuk excursion nine hundred and forty camels along with sixty horses."

Moreover, he brought to the Prophet ﷺ ten thousand dinars, which was at that time a very huge amount of money. The Prophet ﷺ said:

"May Allâh forgive you Uthman for anything you do in public or in secrecy, anything you do till the Day of Resurrection."

This was the way Uthman ﷺ sacrificed for this battle. He offered everything he had to help give the Muslim army power and life. Uthman ﷺ was really trading with Allâh. He was seeking the real forgiveness of Allâh and was looking for a forever-pleasant life in the Hereafter.

Trading with Allâh

Historians reported that during the rule of Abu Bakr ﷺ, people faced great hardships. The land became arid and very few people could find something to eat. The people of Al-Madinah came to Abu Bakr ﷺ and asked him to provide them with something that they could survive with.

However, the Caliph could not do anything to help them. The treasury of the state was empty and there was no other means of filling the empty stomachs. As we have already said, Uthman ﷺ, was a rich merchant. He received a huge caravan from Damascus carrying food and other goods. All the merchants gathered at his house asking him to sell them some of the items he received so that they could sell them to the people. Uthman ﷺ asked them to offer him a good price. The merchants offered high prices, but Uthman ﷺ kept asking for a higher price. He kept telling them that someone had paid him a higher price. When they had offered him the highest price they could, they told him that no merchant could pay more than what they had offered. Uthman ﷺ told them that Allâh had paid him more. For every dirham he will give him ten dirhams. Uthman ﷺ then gave away the whole of the caravan to the poor people of Al-Madinah free of charge.

Rich but Humble

Anyone would think that a man who had all this wealth could surely have led an easy life. However, Uthman ﷺ spent his wealth on providing food for the people, while he himself would eat vinegar and olive oil. Uthman ﷺ was a man who searched for things that were much greater than worldly pleasures. He was seeking the pleasure of Allâh and an eternal life in Paradise.

Uthman ﷺ Elected as the Caliph

'Umar bin Al-Khattab ﷺ, the second Caliph of Islam, was stabbed by a Persian slave named Abu Lu'lu'a. As he was lying on his bed of death, the people around him asked him to appoint a successor. The task was by no means simple, for the small Islamic State had now expanded into an empire. The Persians and Romans received fatal blows and lost large parts of their lands to the Muslims. However, they still formed a threat to the security of the newly founded Islamic State. The internal problems were no less complex. The Muslims had by now become a nation, but some of them were still clinging to tribal customs. The riches brought by conquered lands added to the complexity of the situation. Many Muslims built homes in the conquered lands and stayed there away from the central capital. Islam had come for a different purpose altogether. Its primary aim was not to subdue people, but to guide and reform them. The Caliph to come should protect and promote the religion in addition to his administrative and military responsibilities. These were the problems that 'Umar ﷺ had to face. He could foresee that by time, these duties and problems would increase. So, 'Umar ﷺ left the matter to six prominent Companions of the Prophet ﷺ to elect a new Caliph from amongst themselves. These people were 'Ali bin Abi Tâlib, Az-Zubair bin Al-Awwam, Abdur-Rahman bin Awf, Uthman bin Affan, Talhah bin Ubeidullah and Sa'd bin Abi Waqqas ﷺ.

'Umar ﷺ had directed that the selection of the Caliph should not be delayed beyond the third day after his death. 'Umar's last words of advice to them were:

"Fear Allâh during your rule of people and be just to all."

The six persons met but two days were wasted in unsuccessful attempts to select the Caliph. Abdur-Rahman bin Awf offered to forego his own claim if the others agreed to abide by his decision. All persons agreed to this proposal. So all of them left the matter of electing the new ruler to Abdur-Rahman bin Awf رضي الله عنه after lengthy discussions with senior Companions of the Prophet ﷺ and the final two candidates, Ali رضي الله عنه and Uthman رضي الله عنه, Abdur-Rahman bin Awf رضي الله عنه preferred Uthman رضي الله عنه to 'Ali رضي الله عنه 'Uthman bin Affan رضي الله عنه was finally elected as the new Caliph. At that time, Muslims had become very powerful and rich and Islam began to spread east, north and south. As soon as he was appointed a Caliph, Uthman رضي الله عنه sent a number of letters to his governors and others which indicated the policies he proposed to adopt in governing the state. He told the governors:

> "Allâh has ordered rulers to become protectors of the society and not to become tax collectors. You should take interest in the affairs of Muslims. Even with your enemies your conduct should be upright."

He also wrote to the commanders of armies saying:

> "You are the protectors of Islam against its enemies. You should always be mindful of your conduct."

Conquests under Uthman رضي الله عنه

The conquests made by 'Umar رضي الله عنه in Iraq and Iran had shaken the Persian Empire, but had not destroyed it. There were still some lands in their hands. Some of the lands taken by the Muslims rebelled after the death of Umar رضي الله عنه. Uthman رضي الله عنه directed Al-Waleed bin Uqbah رضي الله عنه, the governor of Kufah in Iraq, to take steps against them. Al-Waleed رضي الله عنه attacked Azerbaijan and its people agreed to pay the tribute again. He sent a force under the command of Salman رضي الله عنه to Armenia, but because of its difficult terrain it could not be completely conquered. The same year, the people of the Ray in Iran had revolted, but they were overpowered by Abu Musa Al-Ash'ari رضي الله عنه. Likewise, there was an uprising in Alexandria, Egypt, which was also put down.

Al-Waleed رضي الله عنه was ordered by Uthman رضي الله عنه to send ten thousand soldiers to Syria under the command of Salman رضي الله عنه to defeat the Romans who attacked the Muslim frontiers. As a result, the Romans lost some of their fortresses. Following their success, the Muslims conquered Asia Minor and established contacts with their forces on the Persian side. From there they went as far as Teflis and to the shores of the Black Sea. In Egypt, Abdullah bin Abi As-Sarh رضي الله عنه carried his arms along the coast beyond Tripoli and Barca and threatened Carthage and the far west. He was met by a huge Roman army. He sent a letter to

Uthman ﷺ asking for reinforcements. Uthman ﷺ sent ten thousand men under the command of Abdullah bin Az-Zubair ﷺ. The outcome of this battle was going to determine the fate of the whole African coast. Uthman ﷺ promised a personal reward of one fifth of the share of the state in the spoils of war. On the other side, the Romans declared a reward of one thousand pounds to anyone killing the Muslim leader. Historians place this battle as the third in magnitude after Qadisiyah and Yarmouk. The Roman Leader was killed by Abdullah bin Az-Zubair ﷺ and the Muslim army gave the Romans a big blow.

As the Islamic State had reached seas and oceans everywhere, there was a great need to establish a fleet of ships in order to help armies cross to the capital of the Byzantine Empire and to spread Islam to Africa and Europe. Mu'awiyah bin Abi Sufyan ﷺ, the governor of Syria, was very eager to establish the fleet. He asked the former Caliph, 'Umar bin Al-Khattab ﷺ, to permit him to build a naval force, but 'Umar ﷺ did not give him permission. Uthman ﷺ finally gave him the permission. The first fleet was equipped in the year 28th after *Hijrah* under the command of Abu Qais ﷺ. The fleet was joined by Abdullah bin Abi As-Sarh ﷺ with other ships manned by Egyptian and Arab warriors. The fleet advanced upon Cyprus which was easily conquered and a large number of men were made captives. On the day of victory, Abu Ad-Darda'a ﷺ, a great Companion of the Prophet ﷺ, burst into tears. Someone asked him the reason for shedding tears, instead of feeling happy and joyful over the event. He replied:

> "These Cypriots were rulers but when they disobeyed Allâh and ignored His teachings, they were reduced to the

state you see now."

The Byzantines made large preparations to regain their losses. Three years after the fall of Cyprus they gathered a fleet of five to six hundred war ships and attacked the Muslims at sea. Abdullah bin Abi As-Sarh ﷺ took the challenge, and with a force much less in number and equipment, but manned by brave warriors could defeat the Byzantines. Before the battle took place, the Muslims spent the whole night in prayers and recitation of Qur'ân while the Greeks kept on chiming their bells. In the morning, the Greeks could not withstand the Muslims' attack and fled. Under the rule of Uthman ﷺ Muslims expanded the Islamic State in every direction. Many of the inhabitants of the conquered lands accepted Islam. Those who kept their religions were treated justly and mercifully.

Virtues and Morals of Uthman ﷺ

Collection of the Noble Qur'ân

During the rule of Uthman ﷺ, many nations accepted the religion of Islam. They spoke different languages and dialects. In addition, dialects began affecting the standard Arabic language. Uthman ﷺ was very keen to keep the language of the Qur'ân as it had purely been revealed from Allâh. He was worried when he realized that the people throughout the parts of the empire were reading the Qur'ân in different dialects. Uthman ﷺ had all the copies of the Qur'ân available at the time collected. He then chose four prominent Companions and got them to compile the Qur'ân in the dialect of the Quraish. Upon completing the job, Uthman ﷺ sent a copy to each side of the empire and ordered them to destroy any other copies of the Qur'ân.

Simplicity

Uthman's life, even after becoming the Caliph, was simple. Although he was one of the richest merchants of Makkah, he did not indulge in pleasures or luxury. He used to take simple food and to put on neat but simple clothes. He also used to do his personal work himself.

Generosity

Uthman's generosity was unlimited. Before assuming the office of the Caliphate, he always helped the Islamic movement by his wealth and bounty. On two special occasions, he proved to be the most generous man on earth at that time. On the first occasion, he equipped the major part of the Muslim army heading to Tabuk and on the second, he distributed all his caravan to the poor and needy and refused to sell it to merchants for high prices. Uthman ﷺ used to give alms and charity freely and to look after widows and orphans. It was his custom to free a slave every Friday. During his period of rule, he did not take any salary for the position.

Patience and Endurance

His patience was unparalleled. In all the hardships he met during his rule, he never lost his poise and tranquility. He resigned himself completely to the Decree of Allâh. His trust in Allâh was unshakable and he acted without concern for his personal safety.

Fear of Allâh

Fear of Allâh guided Uthman's actions. He was always mindful of death, the grave and reckoning on the Day of Judgment. He used to repeat the Prophet's saying:

> "The grave is the first step of the life beyond. If one could pass this stage successfully, other stages would be rendered easy. But if it proved difficult, all other stages would be difficult."

Love of the Prophet ﷺ

Uthman ﷺ loved the Prophet ﷺ dearly. He followed the teachings of the Prophet ﷺ exactly and took them as a source of guidance. He had great regard for the members of the Prophet's family. As a Caliph, he doubled the allowance of the Prophet's widows.

The Rebellion and the End

As the Islamic state expanded greatly under the rule of Uthman ﷺ, many hypocrites who pretended to have accepted Islam worked out plots to disrupt the Muslim nation and destroy the state. They tried all means to make people revolt against Uthman ﷺ. They told people lies about the wealth of Uthman ﷺ and his relatives. Some rebels started moving the still waters here and there. Finally, they gathered thousands against Uthman ﷺ. Although he had the power to stop them and put an end to their plots, he refused all consultations to wage a war against the rebels. Uthman ﷺ was eighty-two years old at that time. He did not like to shed blood. He was always known to be bashful and merciful. He did not expect the people to revolt against him. However, he knew that the Jews were behind the intrigue.

Accusations against Uthman ﷺ

Near the end of Uthman's rule, the move of rebellion in Kufah and Egypt was about to end in turmoil. The enemies of the Caliph began to talk loosely that the Caliph was not following the teachings of the Prophet ﷺ and the preceding Caliphs.

Few people realized the bad consequences of such talks and rumors. In fact, Uthman ﷺ did several things that the rebels took as a false evidence against him. They said that he erected tents in Mina as a shelter during *Hajj* time, the thing which had not been done before. Indeed, the Muslim army used these tents in Mina when they saw other armies using them. It was something trivial to rely on to kill a Caliph. These tents were meant to protect Muslims against the scorching sun. The second allegation of the rebels was that at the time of the Prophet ﷺ and the first two Caliphs, *Zakât* was not levied on horses, while Uthman ﷺ levied *Zakât* on horses.

The fact is that horses had been few and used only in warfare at the time of the Prophet ﷺ. After the wealth that the Muslims gained, Uthman ﷺ saw it was proper to levy *Zakât* on horses as on camels. Many other accusations were made against Uthman ﷺ. The hypocrite Abdullah bin Saba', originally a Jew pretending to have become a Muslim, poured oil on the fire. He did his best to gain his objective, which was to destroy Islam and the Muslim State. He made an allegiance with other governors who were discontent with Uthman ﷺ and the trouble moved to Al-Madinah. However, all those lies against Uthman ﷺ could not change him.

He continued to be a merciful and lenient governor. Even during the time he was attacked by his opponents who wanted to kill him, he did not use the funds of the treasury to spend on those who would guard his house. His enemies told the people that Uthman ﷺ gave more power to his relatives who in turn abused their positions and oppressed those under their rule. The opposition grew to the extent that it spread all over the Islamic State. The people that began all the plotting against him surrounded his house and encouraged people to kill him. Many of his advisors asked him to try putting a stop to the riot but he did not. At last, his opponents entered into his house and killed him while he was reciting the Qur'ân. They opened his cabinet to take the money they had falsely accused him of collecting for his relatives. However, they found a box in which there was a piece of paper that said:

"This is Uthman's testimony before Allâh:

In the Name of Allâh, the Most Gracious, the Most Merciful.

Uthman bin Affan ﷺ bears witness that there is no true deity but Allâh and that Muhammad is Allâh's Messenger. Paradise is true and Hell is true, and Allâh will resurrect everyone on the Day of Judgment, for Allâh will never break His promise. He lives by that, dies with that and resurrects believing in that."

His body was kept inside his house for three days until the people of Al-Madinah could bury it. May Allâh be pleased with Uthman ﷺ for the great services he rendered to Islam and Muslims. It was enough for Uthman ﷺ to be praised by the Prophet ﷺ:

"Uthman ﷺ is bashful to the extent that angels get bashful when they see him."

علي بن أبي طالب رضي الله عنه

- رابع الخلفاء الراشدين -

'Ali bin Abi Tâlib رضي الله عنه

The Fourth Caliph of Ialam

The Boy and the Prophet ﷺ

Background

'Ali bin Abi Tâlib ﷺ belonged to the house of Abdul Muttalib of Bani Hashim clan from the Quraish tribe. After the death of Abdul Muttalib, 'Ali's father, Abu Tâlib, became the chief of the clan. He took care of Muhammad when he was only eight years old for the he was an orphan. He lost his father before he was born and lost his mother when he was only six years old. His grandfather, Abdul Muttalib, took care of him but he passed away when Muhammad was only eight years old. Abu Tâlib loved his nephew dearly. When Muhammad ﷺ was twelve years old, Abu Tâlib took him with him to Damascus. When he was twenty-five years old, he married Khadijah رضي الله عنها. Abu Tâlib was not well off. He had several children. Muhammad ﷺ wanted to help his uncle. Hence, he took 'Ali while he was still a child to live under his care. 'Ali was born twelve years before the Prophet ﷺ was blessed with the message of Islam. The Prophet ﷺ used to isolate himself from the society of Makkah to worship Allâh following the precepts of the religion of Ibrahim. 'Ali helped in bringing food to the Prophet ﷺ at a cave called Hira' at a mountain near Makkah during the period when the Prophet ﷺ was praying to Allâh. He also shared with the Prophet ﷺ in his house, food and whole life. Hence, he learned many things from the Prophet ﷺ,

which qualified him to be a true Muslim since his early childhood. 'Ali was greatly impressed by the manner in which the Prophet ﷺ and his wife Khadijah رضي الله عنها performed their prayers. He noticed that they were leading a life different from the one other people of Makkah were leading. He was also impressed by the way the Prophet ﷺ was dealing with others. He noticed how honest, trustworthy and straightforward the Prophet ﷺ was toward all people, both rich and poor.

Introduction to Islam

While Muhammad was worshipping Allâh at the cave of Hira', he received the Angel Gabriel. The Angel told him that he had been chosen by Allâh to preach Islam to his people. The Prophet ﷺ was ordered to preach the religion of Islam when Makkah and the whole Arabian Peninsula were indulging in the worship of idols. In the beginning, Allâh ordered the Prophet ﷺ to preach the message of Islam to his close relatives. The Prophet ﷺ and his wife Khadijah رضي الله عنها kept their worship secret. As 'Ali was living with them in the same house, he knew everything they were doing. Once, he entered the house and saw the Prophet ﷺ and Khadijah رضي الله عنها praying in a way different from the one his people were doing. He inquired about the prayer they were performing. Although he was still very young to get involved in matters of such importance, the Prophet ﷺ told him that Allâh, the only Lord of the universe, sent him to preach Islam to the people. The Prophet ﷺ also explained to 'Ali the principles of Islam and asked him to accept the message of Islam.

'Ali received this invitation with hesitation. He told the Prophet ﷺ that he would ask his father's counsel. The Prophet ﷺ

said to him that if he did not like to accept the religion, he should keep it secret and not tell anybody about it even his father. 'Ali promised to keep the message secret. Knowing how faithful the Prophet ﷺ was, he thought about the invitation very seriously. He was fully convinced that Muhammad ﷺ would not tell him lies or cheat him, especially since he loved him dearly and wished all the best for him. On the next day he came to the Prophet ﷺ to announce that he believed in the religion of Islam. At that time, 'Ali ﷺ was only twelve years old. It is reported that he was the first boy to accept Islam. 'Ali ﷺ asked the Prophet ﷺ to teach him how to pray. Now, all members of the house of the Prophet ﷺ were praying together. 'Ali ﷺ was standing beside the Prophet ﷺ and his wife during prayers and learning more and more about the sublime principles of Islam. He was an eye witness of the revelation of the Noble Qur'ân and memorized the first Verses revealed to the Prophet ﷺ.

Oppression by the Quraish

The Prophet ﷺ continued preaching Islam secretly to his closest relatives. However, he did not realize much success. Only four or five people accepted the message of Islam. His uncles tried their best to dissuade him.

Three years later, he was ordered by Allâh to proclaim Islam in public. 'Ali ﷺ never thought that the Prophet ﷺ would meet such resistance as long as he was calling his people to goodness. However, he was a witness to the insults and oppression that the Prophet ﷺ faced but he was too young to provide any help to him. All he could do was stop the boys whom the pagans instructed to insult the Prophet ﷺ and throw stones and dust at him.

Although 'Ali's father did not accept the Prophet's invitation to Islam, he offered all the protection he could to the Prophet ﷺ. However, Abu Tâlib did not live long after the proclamation of the message of Islam. Khadijah رضي الله عنها also died and left the Prophet ﷺ alone in the face of the troubles that the chiefs of the Quraish were causing to the Prophet ﷺ. 'Ali ﷺ became an orphan while still a young boy. However, he found support and love under the care of the Prophet ﷺ. They both shared happy and difficult times of life.

The Quraish and other tribes living in and around Makkah found that their efforts to stop the message of Islam were useless. They agreed to besiege the Muslims and Bani Hashim in an arid valley and cut all social and commercial relations with them. 'Ali ﷺ and his fellow Muslims suffered much for three long years. The Quraish prevented anyone from providing any food supplies to the Muslims. They wanted them to die out of hunger.

Migration to Abyssinia

The Prophet ﷺ and his Companions, who were mostly weak people and slaves, received all kinds of torture at the hands of the chiefs of the Quraish. Thirteen years of calling to Islam yielded only little success. Therefore, the Prophet ﷺ had to find a shelter for his Companions against the tyranny of the Quraish. He thought that they should leave to Abyssinia. There ruled a just Christian Emperor whom the people of Arabia respected much.

Some of the weak Muslims left Makkah secretly to Abyssinia. They lived there for some time. The chiefs of the Quraish tried their best to get them back to Makkah but they failed. 'Ali did not like to leave the Prophet ﷺ alone. He kept beside the Prophet ﷺ trying his best to defend him and the other followers of Islam.

The Prophet ﷺ continued his struggle to spread the call of Islam among his tribesmen and the towns near Makkah but he faced huge oppression and resistance.

As Abyssinia was considered a temporary shelter for the Muslims, the Prophet ﷺ did not leave Makkah to Abyssinia with his followers. He changed his way of calling to Islam. He began calling Arabs who were visiting Makkah during seasons. A group of men from Yathrib, a town about four hundred kilometers away, visited Makkah. The Prophet ﷺ met them and explained the principles of Islam to them. They consulted among each other whether to accept the call or not. They became sure that the Prophet ﷺ was truthful. They all believed in him. The Prophet ﷺ told them that he needed protection in their city to be able to proclaim Islam. They promised to provide every means of protection needed for the call to continue as destined by Allâh. They also told him that they would come back the next year with their chiefs to make the final agreement with the Prophet ﷺ. The next year seventy men and women from Yathrib visited Makkah and agreed with the Prophet ﷺ to provide all means they had to protect him and his followers. Hence, the Prophet ﷺ asked his followers to leave to Yathrib. All the Companions of the Prophet ﷺ migrated to Yathrib secretly. There they received help and protection. The Prophet ﷺ, Abu Bakr and 'Ali رضي الله عنهما did not leave with the other migrants. They stayed with the Prophet ﷺ in Makkah until orders came down from heaven to the Prophet ﷺ to leave to Yathrib.

The Plot

When the chiefs of the Quraish felt disparate that they would not be able to stop the call of Islam and that all Muslims escaped their hold and tyranny, they gathered and plotted to kill the Prophet ﷺ. They agreed that forty strong young men from all clans should surround the house of the Prophet ﷺ and all share in murdering him. The Angel Gabriel brought news of the plot to the Prophet ﷺ and conveyed orders to him from Allâh to migrate to Yathrib. The Prophet ﷺ told his Companion, Abu Bakr ﷺ, of the plot and asked him to accompany him to Yathrib.

Sublime Sacrifice

'Ali ﷺ hoped to migrate with the Prophet ﷺ, but he ordered him to stay behind. He told him that some people had entrusted him with some of their precious belongings because they, in spite of their rejection of his call to Islam, believed that he was the trust-worthiest man in the tribe. He also asked 'Ali ﷺ to sleep in his bed and cover his body with his blanket during the night when he and his Companion would leave Makkah. 'Ali ﷺ accepted the mission and slept in the Prophet's bed.

The Prophet ﷺ left his house in the midnight. The forty young men were waiting around the house for the time to come to attack Muhammad and murder him. They did not notice that Muhammad had left his house. At the same time, 'Ali ﷺ slept in the Prophet's bed and covered his body with the Prophet's blanket. The young men were now and then peeping through the cracks of the door. They thought that Muhammad did not leave his house and that he was still sleeping in his bed.

When it was time to go in and kill Muhammad, they removed

the bed cover to surprisingly find 'Ali ﷺ and not Muhammad ﷺ in the bed. Had they not removed the cover, they would have killed 'Ali ﷺ thinking that they had killed the Prophet ﷺ. 'Ali ﷺ sacrificed himself for the life of the Prophet ﷺ.

The young men were surprised to see 'Ali ﷺ. They asked him where Muhammad was? 'Ali ﷺ replied that he did not know. They beat and arrested him. After some time they released him. 'Ali ﷺ delivered all properties that had been kept with the Prophet ﷺ as trusts to their owners and left Makkah to Yathrib. In Al-Madinah (Yathrib), the Prophet ﷺ fostered ties of Islamic brotherhood among the *Muhajireen* and the *Ansâr* (emigrants and supporters). Every emigrant was made the brother in Islam of a supporter. The Prophet ﷺ took 'Ali ﷺ as his brother in Islam. He also told them that whoever loved the Prophet ﷺ should love 'Ali and whoever hurt 'Ali would hurt the Prophet ﷺ. He also said:

"Who would be loyal to 'Ali would be loyal to me."

A new stage of Struggle

Now 'Ali ﷺ was twenty-five years old. He did his best to help in building the first mosque in the new Islamic State. To earn his living, 'Ali ﷺ was drawing water from wells to irrigate farms of Al-Madinah.

Permission to fight the Disbelievers

Immediately after settling in Al-Madinah, the Prophet ﷺ and his Companions began establishing firm foundations for their new Islamic State. At the same time, they were permitted by Allâh to fight the pagans and spread the light of Islam around Al-Madinah. The Muslims began patrolling outside Al-Madinah for security purposes. They received the news that a trade caravan belonging to the Quraish was bound to Makkah back from Damasucs nearby Al-Madinah. They went towards it to check it. Abu Sufyan the leader of the caravan, got the news of Muslims coming towards them, and in fear of their attack, he changed his direction and managed to escape the Muslims. When the Quraish knew of the threat, they prepared a well-armed army of one thousand soldiers and headed to Al-Madinah to destroy the new state of Islam. The Muslims, on the other hand, prepared an army one third the number of the Quraish army with little arms. Both armies met at a place called Badr near Al-Madinah.

The Lion of Allâh

As usual, the pagans requested individual combat between heroes of the two armies. Three strong men from the Quraish army advanced and challenged the Muslims. Three Muslims from the supporters advanced and accepted the challenge. However, the three Makkans refused to fight them and asked for three men from the emigrants. 'Ali رضي الله عنه with two other emigrants advanced and challenged the Makkans. In no time, 'Ali رضي الله عنه killed his opponent. The battle started fiercely. 'Ali رضي الله عنه was known for his courage and skill in combat. He killed several pagan heroes and took several prisoners of war. The battled ended with a great victory for the Muslims and utter defeat for the pagans. 'Ali رضي الله عنه and his fellow Muslims returned to Al-Madinah to continue their struggle for building the Islamic State.

Marriage to Fâtimah رضي الله عنها

In the same year, the Prophet ﷺ accepted for his daughter,

Fâtimah رضي الله عنها, to be betrothed to 'Ali ﷺ. Eleven months later, 'Ali ﷺ and Fâtimah got married. All that 'Ali ﷺ could offer as a dowry was his armor which he had sold for five hundred and eighty dirhams. The Prophet ﷺ gave to his daughter an ordinary cot, a mattress stuffed with palm leaves, a water bag, two grinding stones and two earthen pitchers.

The pure Family

Although they were very poor, 'Ali and Fâtimah رضي الله عنهما led a happy life. Allâh praised this family in the Qur'ân for their self-denial. They were having their meal. The meal consisted of dry bread. A beggar knocked the door and asked for some food. They gave him the dry bread and kept hungry. Although they were very poor, they preferred to give the beggar their food to satisfy their Lord. During peace times, 'Ali earned his living from irrigation of farms in Al-Madinah. The family had their first child and named him Al-Hasan. The child was loved dearly by his family and the Prophet ﷺ.

The pagans attack Again

The pagans did not accept the awful defeat they received at the battle of Badr. They collected their whole energy and wealth and began preparations for another attack against the Muslims. With a force of three thousand men under the command of Abu Sufyan they marched toward Al-Madinah. They were determined to destroy the new state of Islam and bring the Muslims back to Makkah as slaves.

In the first clash of arms the Muslims got the upper hand in spite of the fact that they were less than one third the number of the Quraish army. 'Ali ﷺ fought a big battle and held fast to his position. The archers, whom the Prophet ﷺ placed on top of a small hill behind the Muslim army to protect their backs, saw the pagans flee from the battlefield. They left their positions and began collecting war booty. The course of the battle changed when the Quraish horsemen climbed the hill and killed the remaining archers. Mus'ab bin 'Umair, the banner holder, fell down but 'Ali took the banner and raised it high. He defended the Prophet ﷺ and his Companions to the last minute of the battle. Although the pagans won this battle, they did not achieve their objectives of destroying the state of Islam. 'Ali was very sad to lose his uncle, Hamza, who was a great hero of Islam. He came back to Al-Madinah sad for the loss of the battle but he kept determined to protect his religion and leader.

More attempts to destroy Islam

In the third attempt, the Quraish and their allies gathered an army of ten thousand soldiers and marched toward Al-Madinah. The Muslims were not strong enough to fight an open battle against such a huge army. Therefore, they dug a trench around the city and stood behind it to defend the city against the aggressors. A very brave man from the Quraish challenged the Muslims to an individual combat. 'Ali advanced and accepted the challenge. The man told 'Ali that he did not like to kill a young man like him. However, 'Ali told him that he liked to kill him. Both men engaged in fighting and 'Ali killed the man. The Muslims were very happy to see 'Ali victorious. This event added to the morale of the Muslims and weakened the pagans' stance. 'Ali stood at the side of the trench and dared anybody from the pagans to cross over. Three persons crossed over at a weak point. 'Ali challenged the three men. He killed them one after the other. The siege continued for about one month. Finally, the pagans were forced to leave by a high wind and cold weather. The Muslims were very happy to see the pagans leave the outskirts of their city.

The Treacherous Jews

The Jews of Banu Quraithah broke their agreement of mutual support with the Muslims and shared in the siege. The pagans finally left back to Makkah. As the Muslims were finished with the pagans who left their positions back to their homes, they were ordered by Allâh to punish the traitors. Before taking off his armor, 'Ali ﷺ and the other Muslims accompanied the Prophet ﷺ to the fortress of Banu Quraithah. They besieged the Jews who already cheated the Muslims and refused to support them as they had already agreed. 'Ali ﷺ was the Commander. He kept pressing on the fortress of the Jews until they surrendered. The Prophet ﷺ punished the Jews for their deception and breach of the agreement they held with the Muslims.

The Treaty

After this event, the Prophet ﷺ and his Companions wished to visit Makkah and perform '*Umrah*. Although they wanted their visit to be peaceful, the pagans denied them the right to visit the Ka'bah. After lengthy negotiations at a place called Al-Hudaibiyah, both the Muslims and the pagans agreed to make a peace treaty with each other. 'Ali ﷺ was ordered by the Prophet ﷺ to write the agreement. 'Ali ﷺ started the agreement with the words:

"In the Name of Allâh,

the Most Gracious, the Most Merciful."

The pagans objected to that and told the Prophet ﷺ that they had not believed in the Gracious. They asked the Prophet ﷺ to write 'In the Name of Allâh' only. The Prophet ﷺ ordered 'Ali to write as they requested. 'Ali ؓ then wrote:

This accord is to be held between the Prophet Muhammad ﷺ and the Quraish. They again objected saying that had they accepted him as a Prophet of Allâh, they would not have fought against him. The Prophet ﷺ asked 'Ali ؓ to cross out the words but 'Ali ؓ did not accept to cross out the eternal Truth. The Prophet ﷺ himself crossed out the words.

The man whom Allâh and His Prophet ﷺ Love

The Jews from around Al-Madinah and Khaibar broke all agreements they had made with the Muslims. They supported the pagans and plotted to kill the Prophet ﷺ and weaken the Muslims. They did not like the way Islam was spreading in Arabia. They gathered inside a fortified city called Khaibar near Al-Madinah and began preparations to attack the Muslims. The Prophet ﷺ and his Companions surrounded Khaibar. Several Muslim leaders tried to conquer the city but no one of them came back with victory. On the last day, the Prophet ﷺ said:

"Tomorrow, I will give the banner (leadership) to a man whom Allâh and his Prophet ﷺ love."

All senior Companions of the Prophet ﷺ wished to be the leader. However, the Prophet ﷺ gave the banner to 'Ali ؓ. He led the army to the fortress and challenged their leader named Merhab. In no time, he killed Merhab, opened the gate of the fortress and conquered the town.

Makkah Conquered

The treaty that the Muslims made with the pagans did not stand for long. As usual, the pagans broke their covenants and killed some of the Muslim Alliance. The Prophet ﷺ had no choice but to conquer the city as promised by Allâh. An army of ten thousand Muslims marched toward Makkah. 'Ali ﷺ was a commander of one of the wings of the army. He entered the city peacefully and destroyed the stone idols that were worshipped by the people of Makkah. No one in Makkah was harmed by the Muslim army.

Dearer to the Prophet ﷺ than anybody Else

In the ninth year after emigration to Al-Madinah, the Prophet ﷺ led an army to Tabouk at the northern borders of Arabia to deter the Romans who were conspiring to destroy the Islamic State. He left 'Ali ﷺ behind as a ruler of Al-Madinah while absent. 'Ali ﷺ was not satisfied with this mission. He wanted to join the army. He thought that leaving him behind would be a shame to him. The Prophet ﷺ told him:

" Do you not like to be to me like Hârûn was to Mûsâ عليه السلام?"

'Ali was satisfied with the mission and the position given to him by the Prophet ﷺ.

The Proclamation

On return from Tabouk, The Prophet ﷺ sent the Muslims to Makkah to perform pilgrimage under the leadership of Abu Bakr ﷺ. After the departure of the Muslims to Makkah, *Sûrat*

Al-Taubah (Repentance) was revealed.

The Prophet ﷺ sent 'Ali ﷺ to Makkah to read the proclamation:

"No idolater shall after this year perform pilgrimage. No one shall run round the Ka'bah naked. Who has a treaty with the Prophet ﷺ, it shall continue binding till its end. For the rest, four months are allowed to every man to return to his territory, after which there will exist no obligation on the Prophet ﷺ except towards those people with whom treaties have been made."

The Preacher

In the tenth year after migration, The Prophet ﷺ sent 'Ali ﷺ to preach Islam to the people of Yemen. He did the job very successfully to the extent that the whole Hamadhan tribe accepted Islam. The Prophet ﷺ praised him for the success he achieved in Yemen.

Sad for the loss of the Prophet ﷺ

In the same year, 'Ali ﷺ joined the Prophet ﷺ and the other Muslims in the farewell pilgrimage. After completing the rites of the pilgrimage, the Prophet ﷺ stood at Mina and addressed the Muslims. He told them that the religion of Islam was now complete and perfect and advised them to be good Muslims. Through the speech delivered by the Prophet ﷺ, 'Ali ﷺ guessed that the Prophet ﷺ was going to pass away soon. Upon returning to Al-Madinah, the Prophet ﷺ fell ill. Being the cousin, son-in-law of the Prophet ﷺ and the first Muslim among boys, 'Ali ﷺ kept beside the Prophet ﷺ during his sickness. He saw how hard the fever was on the Prophet ﷺ and how the Prophet ﷺ was patient. After a few days, the Prophet's condition became worse. Abbâs bin Abdul-Muttalib held him by the hand and said to him, "In three days you, by Allâh, will be ruled (by somebody else). And by Allâh, I feel that Allâh's Messenger ﷺ will die from this ailment of his, for I know how the faces of the offspring of 'Abdul-Muttalib look at the time of their death. So let us go to Allâh's Messenger ﷺ and ask him who will take over the caliphate. If it is given to us, we will know it, and if it is given to somebody else, we will request him to tell the new ruler to take care of us." 'Ali ﷺ said, "By Allâh, if we asked Allâh's Messenger ﷺ for it (i.e., The caliphate) and he refused to give it to us, the people will never give it to us after that. And by Allâh, I will not ask Allâh's Messenger ﷺ for it." (*Al-Bukhâri*)

After some days, the Prophet ﷺ passed away like any human being. He elected to be near to his Creator and Lord. 'Ali ﷺ felt very sad for the loss of the Prophet ﷺ. He knew that the nation had lost the man who took it out of darkness to light and that it had now to pave the way for Islam to spread over the world by itself.

'Ali ﷺ was one of three persons who bathed the Prophet's body. He was also one of the persons who went down into the Prophet's grave and placed him in it.

After six months his wife, Fâtimah رضي الله عنها also passed away. Her death added to his sadness. He was left alone in the face of many difficulties. However, he proved to be the man of courage at all times.

'Ali رضي الله عنه Selected as a Caliph

Immediately after the Prophet ﷺ passed away, the Muslims elected Abu Bakr رضي الله عنه as a Caliph. 'Ali رضي الله عنه helped the Caliph in defending the Islamic State especially when the apostates in the Arabian Peninsula threatened to tumble the state.

After Abu Bakr's death, 'Umar رضي الله عنه took over rule upon the recommendation of Abu Bakr رضي الله عنه. 'Ali رضي الله عنه was appointed as a judge. 'Umar رضي الله عنه referred difficult cases to him and took him as his advisor. Before he passed away, 'Umar رضي الله عنه selected six persons among whom was 'Ali رضي الله عنه to select one of them as a Caliph. The majority preferred 'Uthman to 'Ali رضي الله عنه.

During 'Uthman's rule, 'Ali رضي الله عنه continued his efforts to strengthen the Islamic State. He kept beside 'Uthman رضي الله عنه as an advisor. He did his best to make the Islamic State spread over new lands.

Following the murder of 'Uthman رضي الله عنه, the senior Companions insisted that 'Ali رضي الله عنه take over. In the beginning, he did not accept the mission. However, both Az-Zubair and Talhah رضي الله عنهما urged him to accept the position of the fourth Caliph of Islam. They wanted a strong man to stop the rebels and restore order to the state. The conditions of the state were very bad at that time. The people who revolted against and killed 'Uthman رضي الله عنه took hold of Al-Madinah and even led the public prayers. The people of the city gave allegiance to the Caliph. However, several regional rulers refused to pledge loyalty to him. They did not deny Ali's ability to lead and his many virtues. However, they felt that he should have taken a firmer stance against Uthman's murderers.

'Ali ﷺ was confronted with a huge number of problems. The rebels tumbled the life of the society. They were very strong and liked to control the Caliph and the people. However, 'Ali ﷺ wanted to stop them. They requested him to dismiss the rulers who were relatives to 'Uthman ﷺ. 'Ali ﷺ knew that these rulers were not good. He immediately ordered them to give up their positions. The rulers of some provinces also refused to listen to him and held fast their positions.

Some rulers took the case of 'Uthman's murder as an excuse to revolt against the Caliph. They requested the Caliph to kill the people who killed 'Uthman ﷺ. They demanded the killing of the murderers, and in their forcefulness they created problems for the new Caliph.

The situation was very bad for him. He did not like to shed blood and at the same time wanted to stop the corruption of rulers. He asked Mu'awiyah ﷺ to pledge loyalty to him, but Mu'awiyah refused to listen to him. Mu'awiyah asked 'Ali ﷺ to detain the rebels and kill them for killing 'Uthman ﷺ. He resisted 'Ali's control. Unfortunately, the two Companions could not reach a settlement for a long time. Instead of directing the efforts of the government to spread Islam, all resources were being used for suppressing troubles here and there. Finally, both 'Ali and Mu'awiyah رضي الله عنهما agreed to resort to arbitration instead of fighting. They were both keen to keep the Muslim nation strong and unified.

'Ali رضي الله عنه selected Abu Mousa Al-Ash'ari رضي الله عنه as his arbitrator and Mu'awiyah رضي الله عنه selected 'Amr bin Al-'Aas رضي الله عنه as his arbitrator. 'Amr deceived Abu Mousa Al-Ash'ari رضي الله عنه when both arbitrators agreed to dismiss both Mu'awiyah and 'Ali رضي الله عنهما and to leave it to the nation to select a ruler. Abu Mousa came out to the people and declared that he dismissed 'Ali رضي الله عنه. However, 'Amr رضي الله عنه told the people that he supported Mu'awiyah رضي الله عنه. Hence, settlement was not achieved and the troubles for the Caliph continued.

In addition to these troubles, some of 'Ali's supporters revolted against him because he accepted arbitration. They were fanatics. They also claimed that 'Ali رضي الله عنه had become a disbeliever when he accepted arbitration. The Khawarej (dissidents) killed anyone who supported 'Ali's point of view. 'Ali رضي الله عنه did his best to bring them back to the fold of Islam peacefully but without success. Hence, he had no choice but to fight them and stop their aggression against people.

As a result of all these troubles, three of the dissidents agreed to kill 'Ali, Mu'awiyah and 'Amr رضي الله عنهم. Each one of them prepared himself well for the evil job. One named Abdur-Rahman bin Muljim, whom 'Ali رضي الله عنه was very kind to during past days, came to the mosque and hid in it. He knew that 'Ali رضي الله عنه would come to the *Fajr* (dawn) paryer. As 'Ali رضي الله عنه started performing prayer, the man came forward and stabbed him several times with a dagger. The people behind him caught the murderer and carried 'Ali رضي الله عنه home. Three days later 'Ali رضي الله عنه passed away leaving the nation in the eye of the storm.

'Ali's rule continued for four years and nine months. The majority of historians confirm that he died at the age of sixty-three. His sons Al-Hasan and Al-Husain رضي الله عنهما buried him. The whole nation was disturbed by the death of this great Companion of the Prophet ﷺ.

Hence, the period of 'Ali's rule was full of troubles for him and for the Muslims in general. During this period no new lands were added to the Islamic State. The Caliph was busy trying to bring order to the state itself. The differences among the Muslims killed any chance of conquest.

Following 'Ali's death, Mu'awiyah ﷺ restored order to the state and became the Caliph.

Virtues of 'Ali bin Abi Tâlib ﷺ

Simplicity

'Ali ﷺ lived a simple life. Till the age of twenty-five or twenty-six he had lived with the Prophet ﷺ and had tried to imitate him in every way. His household was so simple that it consisted of few items. He gave his guests dinner on his wedding day only by selling his armour. Fatimah رضي الله عنها was doing all her housework and 'Ali ﷺ was helping her now and then. He was earning his living by doing manual work like drawing water for irrigation. There were many days in his life when he went without meals. When he became a Caliph, he did not change his simple way of life. He continued putting on the most ordinary clothes and taking the simplest possible food. All that he used to take was a cup of milk, a piece of barley bread and some vegetables. He always told his companions that a Caliph was only entitled to two dishes, one for him and his family and the other for the poor. He continued living in the same small house and did not build any house of his own. No guard was kept at the house and there was nothing to distinguish it from those of poor people.

Simplicity was the keynote of his life. Even as a Caliph, he did not feel shy of doing manual labour even mending his shoes. He would sit on the ground and even go to sleep on the bare floor. A goat-skin served as the rug of his house on which he received envoys and distinguished persons.

Generosity

Although 'Ali ﷺ was very poor and barely had adequate living, he would never let any poor man go disappointed from his door. In his early days, he once irrigated an orchard throughout the night to earn some barley. He divided the barley into three portions and had a portion cooked. When the meal was ready a beggar came and 'Ali ﷺ gave all of the food to him. He had the second portion cooked when an orphan turned up and the food was given to him. The third portion went to a prisoner. He was ever ready to help the weak and to redress the wrongs of the oppressed.

Courage

'Ali ﷺ was unsurpassed in terms of bravery. He had given a glorious example of it in every battle he fought. In Badr, he killed his opponent in individual combat. He also killed several pagan heroes to the extent that he emerged as the hero of the battle. In the battle of Uhud, he also killed the man from the enemy army who challenged him to an individual combat. Likewise in the Trench Battle, he advanced to challenge a renowned hero and killed him. His bravery earned him the title of 'Lion of Allâh.'

In all other battles, 'Ali ﷺ proved to be the man whom the Prophet ﷺ and the Muslims could rely on. Khaibar town stood fast in the face of several Muslim commanders but when the mission was given to 'Ali ﷺ, it could not stand. He also kept close to the Prophet ﷺ in all battles and never retreated.

Treatment of Enemies

The Prophet ﷺ said:

"Strong is not he who overpowers his foe, but one who restrains his temper."

'Ali ﷺ was a living example of this precept. He overpowered many foes, but he did not ill-treat any enemy. In an individual combat he had once thrown down his enemy and was on the point of cutting off his head when the desperate foe spat on his face. 'Ali ﷺ spared his life and let him go. When asked to explain his strange conduct, 'Ali ﷺ said that if he had killed his enemy after spitting on his face, his motive would not have remained purely for the cause of Allâh but due to personal anger. In another combat, he left his enemy when he fell down naked. Although Az-Zubair bin Al-'Awwam ﷺ stood against him, he wept when he received news that he had been killed. He said Announce the penalty of Hellfire to the killer of Saifyah's son. I had heard from the Prophet ﷺ saying:

"Every Prophet ﷺ had a disciple and Az-Zubair is my disciple."

He was merciful even to his killer. He ordered his sons to offer him food and let him sleep on a soft bed.

Justice

'Ali ﷺ was known for his acute sense of justice. Whatever was received in the treasury he used to distribute equitably and would not even listen to the request of his brother 'Aqeel ﷺ to give him a little more share. 'Abdullah bin Mas'ud ﷺ as well as 'Umar ﷺ used to say that 'Ali ﷺ was the best judge.

Once an interesting case had came before him. Two persons

had sat down together to take a meal. One had five loaves and the other had three loaves. When they were about to start eating they were joined by a third person. The loaves were put together and all the three ate the meal. The third person gave eight coins and went away. The man who had five loaves took five coins and gave three to the other. The latter insisted on equal distribution and the matter came up before 'Ali ﷺ. He advised the man to accept what was offered to him as it was profitable for him but he demanded justice. 'Ali ﷺ then announced that seven coins should be retained by the man who had five loaves and the other man should be given one coin. The latter's objection to this judgment was refuted when 'Ali ﷺ explained the reason for his decision. He stated that every loaf should have been divided in three parts. Thus the man with three loaves had nine parts and the total would be twenty-four parts. As three persons had shared the meal, it should be taken that every man had eaten eight parts of the loaves. Thus the second man had himself taken eight of his nine parts of loaves while the first one had contributed seven. The first one should therefore get seven coins and the second should get only one.

Learning

'Ali ﷺ memorized the Qur'ân by heart. He knew pricesly when, where and in what conditions most Verses of the Qur'ân were revealed. He was considered among the top interpreters of the Noble Qur'ân. For thirty years he was a constant companion of the Prophet ﷺ and therefore he was well versed in a large number of the Prophet's sayings. Even in the time of earlier Caliphs he used to give lectures on the Noble Qur'ân and *Hadith* (Prophet's sayings). Abu Bakr,

'Umar, 'Uthman and 'Aishah ﷺ used to refer difficult cases to him for decision.

'Ali ﷺ was also an orator of the highest order. He could deliver highly inspiring speeches before any audience.

Religious life

'Ali ﷺ paid much attention to not only obligatory prayers but also to *Nawafil* (additional prayers). Often he would spend whole nights in prayer and used to get so absorbed in them that nothing else mattered. In the battle Uhud an arrow had deeply pierced his leg. It was removed when 'Ali ﷺ stood up for prayers and he did not show any signs of pain at the time of its extraction.

Wisdom and Eloquence

'Ali ﷺ was known to be very wise. Many of the cases referred to him were very difficult but he could always solve them. 'Umar bin Al-Khattab ﷺ always consulted him in cases of *Shari'ah* (Islamic law). In addition 'Ali ﷺ was one of the most eloquent Arabs. He delivered about five hundred speeches. He also made many statements which Arabs still reiterate in their speech. Some of them were taken as proverbs. Examples of such statements are:

Like for others the things you like for yourself.

Do not treat others with injustice as you do not like others to treat you with injustice.

Do not take your friend's enemy as your friend.

He who makes good his inner intentions, Allâh would make good his outer appearance.

He once described the Noble Qur'ân as follows:

"You should learn that this Qur'ân is the sincere advisor, the guide that never leads you astray and the speaker that never lies. Anyone who reads the Qur'ân would benefit of it ...."

He also advised his son saying:

"Profession with adequacy is better than richness with injustice. You should keep your secret within yourself. Keep company with good people and keep away from bad people. The worst food you take is the one you earn in a forbidden way. Be kind to anyone who might be harsh to you, for after a while he would become kind to you."

All in all, practice of justice, self-denial, honesty, purity and love of truth were the hallmarks of 'Ali's character. He never looked at worldly things with admiration. He considered this life as a farm for the life to come. He always wanted to grow good deeds to receive the fruits of them on the Day of Judgment.

He holds a very high position in the hearts and minds of all Muslims. They all remember him with respect and admiration for his long struggle for the cause of Islam and for his kinship to the Prophet ﷺ.

The Prophet ﷺ said to 'Ali ﷺ:

"You are my brother in this life and the life to come."

'Abdullah bin 'Abbas رضي الله عنهما said about him:

"May Allâh be pleased with him. He was the banner of guidance, the shelter of piety, the most wise and the best in holding to the true faith of Islam. He was the best believer, the most eloquent and the most generous and the husband to the best and purest woman."

The End

The days of 'Ali's reign were troublesome. His life was a continuous struggle and he had hardly a moment of peace. To increase his difficulties, when Ibn Muljin slabbed him on his head and side, he said to his son:

> "Treat the man kindly and give him food and water. If I die, his life is left to justice, and he shall be slain for the deed he had done; but do not mutilate him, for that was forbidden by the Prophet ﷺ."

As his condition deteriorated people asked him if he would like his son Al-Hasan ﵁ to succeed him. As 'Ali ﵁ was true to the principle of consultation, he replied:

> "I do not commend this, neither do I forbid it. You better decide for yourself."

He then called his sons, Al-Hasan and Al-Husain to his bedside and advised them to be steadfast in piety and submission to the Will of Allâh. He dictated his testament and continued repeating the Name of Allâh. He breathed his last breath on Friday the 20th of Ramadhân in the year 40 after the Hijrah. All the Muslims were very sad to learn that 'Ali ﵁ was killed. However, 'Ali ﵁ had always asked Allâh to die as a martyr for the Cause of Islam. Allâh accepted his prayers.

May Allâh bestow his mercy on 'Ali ﵁ for his full dedication to the welfare of Islam and the Muslims.

أبو عبيدة بن الجراح رضي الله عنه

ـ أمـــين الأمـــة ـ

Abu 'Ubaidah bin Al-Jarrah رضي الله عنه

The Nation's Trustworthy Man

Side by Side with the Prophet ﷺ

Background

In spite of the corrupt atmosphere that loomed over Makkah before the advent of Islam, Abu 'Ubaidah led a life of honesty and humility. He resented the practices of pagans of Makkans and decided to keep pure and straightforward. He spent most of his time thinking of the gloom that prevailed over his society and of a way out of such darkness.

Even when he was invited by his peers to join them in fun and trivial pleasures, he preferred to keep clean and resorted to thinking about the universe and creation.

As soon as he learnt that the Prophet ﷺ was calling people to adopt a new way of life guided by Allâh, he positively responded to the message and embraced Islam.

With deep thinking, he compared the values and morals the Prophet ﷺ was preaching to the false and misguided life which the pagans were leading. He truly knew that the idols his tribesmen were worshipping were false deities. They could not offer him any good nor cause him any harm. He believed that worshipping these idols reduced the value of reason down to the level of animals.

Islam introduced to Abu 'Ubaidah

Abu 'Ubaidah was a close friend of Abu Bakr ﷺ, who was

the first man to believe in Islam. As soon as Abu Bakr ﷺ explained to him the values and faith the Prophet ﷺ was preaching, he asked his friend to arrange a meeting with the Prophet ﷺ to hear from him directly.

Upon seeing the Prophet ﷺ and hearing the Qur'ân, Abu 'Ubaidah realized that this man was not the type of person the pagans claimed him to be. He had heard them saying that Muhammad ﷺ was an enchanted man, a lunatic or a poet. They tried their best to convince others that the words the Muhammad ﷺ was uttering were inspired by underworld spirits. However, they could never reach a clear explanation of the case because they were under the veil of gloom that controlled their minds and souls.

In spite of all the troubles and pressures he foresaw to befall him, Abu 'Ubaidah ﷺ embraced Islam and kept side by side with the Prophet ﷺ during this difficult period in the history of Islam. He liked the Prophet ﷺ and the new religion more than he liked himself, his family and the whole world.

Endurance

As Islam was growing inside Makkah with difficulty, the new Muslims were day after day facing more oppression and harassment to make them recant. Abu 'Ubaidah had his share of agonies that made him more steadfast and more persevering. He saw how much the Prophet ﷺ was suffering in the process of calling the Makkans to Islam.

When all ways had failed to defame Islam and the Prophet ﷺ, the pagans started a new method of physical torture against weak Muslims. All the Muslims, including Abu 'Ubaidah ﷺ

accepted the challenge and kept patient in spite of all agonies they faced.

Migration to Abyssinia

However, the Muslims felt that they could not continue their message in such a gloomy environment and under such oppression. Hence, they asked the Prophet ﷺ to find a way to put an end to the atrocities inflicted on them by the pagans. The Prophet ﷺ asked them to leave to Abyssinia where they could find shelter. Abu 'Ubaidah ﷺ found it improper to leave the Prophet ﷺ to face the oppressors alone. He decided to stay in Makkah.

The Siege

When the Quraish used up all ways to put out the light of Islam, they decided to impose a boycott against the Muslims and Bani Hashim, the clan to which the Prophet ﷺ belonged. They besieged them within a valley called *Sha'bah Abi Tâlib* (Abu Tâlib's valley). They also wrote a pledge among themselves to cut all commercial and familial relations with the Muslims and to deprive them any source of food.

The Prophet ﷺ, Abu 'Ubaidah ﷺ and other Muslims spent three tough years under the siege. They even ate everything they could find including bones and leaves of trees. However, they remained steadfast to their faith and never retreated.

The siege failed at last, but oppression continued. The Muslims were too weak to challenge the Quraish. Therefore, the Prophet ﷺ instructed his Companions to migrate to Abyssinia for the second time. Abu 'Ubaidah ﷺ and many other Muslims left Makkah to the new land to seek refuge against the oppression of the pagans.

The pagans, on the other hand, felt very angry to see the Muslims have escaped themselves. Therefore, they decided to get them back from Abyssinia. They sent an envoy to the emperor of Abyssinia to convince him to surrender the persons who had sought refuge in his land.

The envoy plotted to entice the emperor against the Muslims. He told the emperor that these people left the religion of their forefathers and resented all religions including Christianity. The emperor was a wise and just man. He brought the Muslims before him. He asked them to refute the allegations made against them. The representative of the Muslims, Ja'far bin Abi Tâlib ﷺ, explained to the emperor their situation before and after the rise of Islam. He also told the emperor that they believed that Jesus Christ was son the of Mary and a Prophet. The emperor was convinced that this group of Muslims were following the true religion. He told them that they were free to live in his land and that nobody would cause them any harm. The refugees found there much care and love and stayed several years until the Prophet ﷺ and his followers migrated to Al-Madinah.

Emigration to Al-Madinah

The Prophet ﷺ and his followers faced many hardships in Makkah. He did his best to find a shelter for the Muslims to live in peace and worship Allâh the way they liked. He went to the market every day and presented his message to visitors from outside of Makkah. However, the Quraish chiefs were always following his steps to fail his plans.

One day, the Prophet ﷺ met some visitors from a town about four hundred kilometers away from Makkah called Yathrib. He explained Islam to them and convinced them to accept it.

The Jews in the suburbs of Yathrib had always threatened the two tribes of Al-Aws and Al-Khazraj, who inhabited Yathrib, that a Prophet from the Arab land was going to appear soon. They told them that they would follow his religion and put the Arabs to sword.

So, the Prophet ﷺ asked the group from Yathrib to provide him protection in their town so he could propagate the message of Islam. The group promised him to come back next year and conclude a pledge of loyalty with him.

The said pledge would provide protection for the Prophet ﷺ and his Companions if they migrated to Al-Madinah. Hence, the Prophet ﷺ commanded his Companions to migrate to that town.

Muslims' Reunion

Upon receiving news that the Prophet ﷺ and the other Muslims escaped the Quraish and migrated to Al-Madinah, Abu Ubaidah ﷺ and his migrant companions left Abyssinia to join their fellow Muslims in the new Islamic State.

The migrants from Abyssinia were met with warm welcome. The people of Al-Madinah provided them with all means of livelihood and took them as brothers in Islam.

This reunion gave Abu 'Ubaidah ﷺ a chance to share in building the new Islamic State and to exert his best efforts to make it strong and lasting.

He shared with the other Muslims in building the first mosque of Islam and worked hard to foster the faithful relations among brother Muslims.

The Real Test

The Muslims settled in Al-Madinah under the protection of the *Ansâr* (supporters). But the Quraish forced and threatened the polytheists of Al-Madinah to provide help to them against Muslims. Upon this Allâh allowed the Muslims to fight the Quraish in self-defense.

The First battle against the Idolaters

The Muslims began patrolling outside Al-Madinah for security purposes. They received the news of a Quraish caravan nearby. They went towards it to check it. Abu Sufyan, the leader of the caravan, got the news of Muslims coming towards them, in fear of their attack, he changed his direction and managed to escape the Muslims. At the same time, he sent a warning message to the Quraish that their trade caravan was in danger.

The Quraish chiefs were furious to hear such news. They collected an army of about one thousand men armed to their teeth and marched toward Al-Madinah to rescue the caravan. On their way to Al-Madinah they received news that the caravan escaped the Muslims and that there was no need for them to continue their march.

However, some chiefs of the Quraish were very arrogant. They were intent on undermining the Muslims and Islam. They insisted on continuing their march to stop the threat of the Muslims.

The Muslims received news of the huge army marching to Al-Madinah to put an end to their existence and faith. They were still weak and lacked the resources to fight back. However, the Prophet ﷺ consulted with his followers on the best way to face the threat. At last, they concluded that they should challenge the Quraish in an open battle in spite of the fact that they did not have equal power. They believed that Allâh would not forsake them. Three hundred and thirteen soldiers headed to a place near to Al-Madinah called Badr to meet the army of the Quraish.

Although the army of the Quraish was three times their number with more horses and better arms, the Muslims were determined to fight their first battle against tyranny. Abu 'Ubaidah ﷺ was fully prepared to fight those who caused many harms to him and his comrades. He felt very strong because he believed that Allâh was supporting them.

Faith or Father

The battle started fiercely. Abu 'Ubaidah ﷺ was doing his best to prove that the Muslims were stronger. To his surprise, he saw his father fighting with the army of the Quraish. His father also took notice of him and was determined to kill his son. He had already took an oath that if he met his son, he would not let him live a minute longer. His son had abandoned his gods (idols) and followed the religion of Islam.

Both father and son met face to face. Abu 'Ubaidah's position was so critical. He was hesitant to kill his father. He did his best to avoid his father. It was really a hard test. However, the father insisted on killing his son.

Both father and son exchanged blows. Abu 'Ubaidah ﷺ had no choice but to defend his faith and life. So, he killed his father.

Abu 'Ubaidah ﷺ felt very sad for that. He thought that he did a great sin. However, a Verse of the Noble Qur'ân came down praising his act:

> "You (O Muhammad ﷺ) will not find any people who believe in Allâh and the Last Day, making friendship with those who oppose Allâh and His Messenger (Muhammad ﷺ), even though they were their fathers or their sons or their brothers or their kindred (people). For such he has written Faith in their hearts, and strengthened them with *Rûh* from Himself." (58:22)

Now Abu 'Ubaidah ﷺ was satisfied that he did the right thing. He knew that to defend his faith was better than to keep good relations with his disbelieving father.

More Challenges, more Perseverance!

Two years later, Abu 'Ubaidah ﷺ had to face another challenge. The Quraish chiefs received a big defeat in the battle of Badr. Therefore, they decided to revenge themselves on the Muslims. They gathered a huge army of three thousand soldiers including their allies and marched to Al-Madinah with an objective to fight their last battle against the Muslims.

The Muslims discussed the threat. Some of them thought it would be better to keep inside Al-Madinah and defend it against invaders. Others, however, saw that they should not give the pagans any idea that they feared to fight them in an open battle. Finally, it was decided to fight the invaders in an open battle.

The Muslims gathered an army of one thousand men and headed to Uhud Mount to challenge their enemies. However, some hypocrites, who had already chosen to keep inside Al-Madinah, withdrew about one third of the army and left back to Al-Madinah. The Muslims were in a very critical position but they strongly believed in Allâh's support.

The Prophet ﷺ commanded fifty archers to take their positions over a small mount near the battle scene to protect the backs of the Muslim army. He ordered them to hold to their positions whatever the result of the battle might be.

The Defeat

As the battle started, the pagans began fleeing the battle scene and Muslims were behind them. It was about to be a striking defeat to the pagans. The archers saw their fellow Muslims collecting spoils of the defeated army. Most of them, against the orders of their Commander, left their positions and joined others in collecting the booty. Some horsemen of the Quraish army were closely watching the archers leaving their positions. They climbed the mount and killed the remaining archers. They attacked the backs of the Muslim soldiers. The fleeing soldiers of the Quraish took notice of the attack and recovered their morale. They counter attacked the Muslims from the other side. They surrounded the Muslims. The initiative was now in their hands. Many of the Muslim fighters were killed while others escaped the battle scene to Al-Madinah. They thought that the Prophet ﷺ was killed. Others, however, held to their positions and fought a disparate battle.

Better to die than Surrender

Abu 'Ubaidah ﷺ was among the soldiers who insisted on fighting to the last moment. He was keen to protect his faith and the Prophet ﷺ who took him out of the gloom that was surrounding him. He stood by the Prophet ﷺ and other Companions fighting with all his might. He was astonished to see an arrow hit the Prophet's face. The Prophet ﷺ fell down and was about to be killed. Abu 'Ubaidah ﷺ ran toward the Prophet ﷺ. He saw two chains of the Prophet's armor going into the cheeks of the Prophet ﷺ. In such a terrible situation, Abu 'Ubaidah ﷺ had no time to look for options. He bit the chains with his front teeth and removed them out of the Prophet's face. In doing so he lost his own two front teeth. However, he continued defending the Prophet ﷺ until the end of the battle.

The Trench

Abu 'Ubaidah ﷺ was also one of the Muslims who shared in digging the trench to protect Al-Madinah against the pagans. The pagans gathered from all parts of the Arabian Peninsula to give Islam and the Muslims the final and fatal blow. Abu 'Ubaidah ﷺ spent many days and nights guarding the weak points of the trench lest any of the confederates' soldiers tried to cross over the trench and attack Al-Madinah. He was a witness to how much the Prophet ﷺ trusted that Allâh would not leave them alone in the confrontation and how much the Prophet ﷺ was confident that Islam would spread all over the world. He heard the Prophet ﷺ saying when he was breaking the rocks that hindered the progress of work:

"Allâh is the greatest, I have been given the keys of Syria, Persia and Yemen."

The Military Commander

Abu 'Ubaidah ﷺ was commissioned by the Prophet ﷺ to lead many military efforts against the Arabs who were plotting to harm the Muslims and stop the spread of Islam. In all such efforts, he proved to be the loyal and faithful soldier.

Some of the Arab tribes around Al-Madinah were now and then trying to harm the Muslims. The Prophet ﷺ commissioned Abu 'Ubaidah ﷺ to put an end to their assaults against the properties of the Muslims. Abu 'Ubaidah ﷺ with his companions stopped their offences.

He was also commissioned by the Prophet ﷺ to intercept a caravan of the Quraish near the seashore. They waited for the caravan for a long time. Their supply of food vanished. Hence, they were forced to eat tree leaves and grass. At last, Allâh brought them a huge whale by the shore. They kept eating from the whale until they became fat. They brought some meat when they came back to Al-Madinah and gave the Prophet ﷺ some of it.

The Romans on the northern borders of Arabia tried to conclude a pact of allegiance with the Quda'a tribes to cause disruption to the Muslim state. The Prophet ﷺ commissioned 'Amr bin Al-'Aas ﷺ to fight them. 'Amr ﷺ saw that he, with the small group of fighters, could not fight the enemy. He sent an envoy to the Prophet ﷺ asking for support. The Prophet ﷺ commissioned Abu 'Ubaidah ﷺ to lead two hundred soldiers to support the fighters led by 'Amr bin Al- 'Aas ﷺ. When both groups met together, 'Amr bin Al-'Aas ﷺ told Abu 'Ubaidah ﷺ that he was the first to lead the army and that Abu 'Ubaidah ﷺ was sent as support to him. Abu 'Ubaidah ﷺ, although he preceded 'Amr in accepting Islam, did not object to Amr's words. He did not object to being like any soldier in the army as long as the objective was to spread the Word of Allâh.

Abu 'Ubaidah ﷺ joined the Prophet ﷺ and the Muslims in every military or civil effort in support of Islam and the Muslims. He took part in the battle to conquer Khaịbar and expel the Jews who were always conspiring to destroy the message of Islam.

Even when other leaders contested his leadership, he humbly gave them all the power they wanted because he considered himself fighting for a greater and more sublime objective than mere power and authority.

Back to the Homeland

The Muslims and the Quraish held a truce for a period of ten years. The agreement provided peace for both sides and brought many tribes and clans to Islam.

The Quraish broke its promise of stopping war against the Muslims for ten years. They attacked some Muslims and killed them. The Prophet ﷺ was now ready to conquer Makkah. He prepared a huge army and divided it into wings. His Companions marched toward Makkah. Abu 'Ubaidah ﷺ led one of those unarmed factions and entered Makkah in a peaceful manner. First, he thought that the Prophet ﷺ would revenge himself against those who stood against him. However, he highly admired the acts of the Prophet ﷺ. He saw how much the Prophet ﷺ was merciful to the Makkans who treated him badly, forced him to leave the city which he loved very much and fought many battles against him with the intent to destroy his Message and undermine his new born state. He entered

Makkah leading thousands of soldiers unarmed to show the Arabs that Islam was not a religion that aimed at killing, but at preaching with mercy.

Abu 'Ubaidah ﷺ shared in all the battles that the Prophet ﷺ initiated against the pagans all over the Arabian Peninsula, to deter them and to stop their aggression against Islam and the Muslims.

He sadly listened to the Prophet ﷺ bidding them farewell and teaching them the final principles of Islam during his farewell address.

The Trustworthy

Abu 'Ubaidah ﷺ was a man of good character and morals. The Prophet ﷺ loved him very much. No one of the followers of the Prophet ﷺ could claim to be as trustworthy in the eyes of the Prophet ﷺ as Abu 'Ubaidah was.

The trusted Envoy

A delegation from Najran came to Al-Madinah to negotiate an agreement with the Prophet ﷺ. They agreed with the Prophet ﷺ to provide them protection for *Jizyah* (a sum of money). After concluding the treaty, They asked the Prophet ﷺ to send one of his Companions to their land to collect the *Jizyah*. They told the Prophet ﷺ that such a man should be trustworthy to the utmost. The Prophet ﷺ told them that he would send a truly trustworthy man with them. All those present were keen to know who was that man whom the Prophet ﷺ meant. It was a great honour for every one of them to be that man.

The next day, many of the Prophet's followers were present in the mosque to perform *Zuhr* (noon prayer). Everyone was eager to know the man whom the Prophet ﷺ considered as the trustworthy. Many of the Companions of the Prophet ﷺ were hoping to have that honour. They listened carefully to the Prophet ﷺ when he called Abu 'Ubaidah ﷺ to assume that huge responsibility. The Prophet ﷺ held Abu

'Ubaidah's hand and said:

> "Every *Ummah* has a trustworthy man; Abu 'Ubaidah ﷺ is the trustworthy man of this *Ummah*."

Sublime Objectives

Abu 'Ubaidah ﷺ was the best example of trust and honesty to the last moment of his life. He was taught by the Prophet ﷺ that nothing in this life is equal to purity of soul and body and that nothing in this life is equal to the promised reward on the Day of Judgment for those who keep honest and trustworthy.

Self Denial

Abu 'Ubaidah ﷺ continued his struggle for the sake of Islam. Whenever the Prophet ﷺ asked him to carry out any mission, he fulfilled such mission properly.

To his grave sorrow, he lost the person who taught him to be a real man of honour and dedication. Some days after the completion of the farewell pilgrimage, the Prophet ﷺ and his followers returned to Al-Madinah to continue their efforts in building their Islamic State. The Prophet ﷺ, however, fell ill and finally passed away like any other human being.

Abu 'Ubaidah ﷺ felt as if the world around him had changed. At first, he could not believe that the Prophet ﷺ had passed away and that the nation was left alone to decide on its future. He was well aware that by the death of the Prophet ﷺ, revelation would cease to come down. However, he was sure that the last Verses of Qur'ân revealed to the Prophet ﷺ made it clear that the religion had now become complete and perfect.

Wisdom and Action

Abu 'Ubaidah ﷺ and other Muslims were busy preparing the body of the Prophet ﷺ to bury it. They suddenly received news that the *Ansâr* had gathered at a place to decide who should be the successor from among them. Leaders of the Muslims feared that such an act would cause differences among the Muslims and result in fighting among the members of the *Ummah* even before the Prophet ﷺ was buried.

Abu Bakr, 'Umar bin Al-Khattab and Abu 'Ubaidah رضي الله عنهم agreed to face the problem and find a solution. They met with the *Ansâr* men and discussed the matter. The *Ansar* first insisted on having the Caliph from among them. Signs of a dispute were about to emerge.

Abu Bakr ﷺ, with his wise mentality, tried to convince them that the Caliph should be from among the Prophet's tribesmen. He took the hands of both 'Umar and Abu 'Ubaidah رضي الله عنهما and told the congregation that they could elect either one to be the Caliph.

As 'Umar ﷺ heard these words, he took his hand off Abu Bakr's hand and told him that no one should be the Caliph other than Abu Bakr ﷺ. He was the first to believe in Islam, the best believer and the one who sacrificed all he could to firmly establish Islam.

Abu 'Ubaidah ﷺ, on the other hand, wept and told Abu Bakr ﷺ that it was shameful for him to be put in a position superior to the first believer and closest follower of the Prophet ﷺ. He absolutely rejected to be elected as Caliph and preferred to remain a humble member of the Islamic *Ummah*.

Both 'Umar and Abu 'Ubaidah رضي الله عنهما took the hand of Abu Bakr ﷺ and pledged to obey him in everything he said or did. By this action, all other Muslims, both emigrants and supporters, were convinced that the best man was elected for the position of the Caliph. They all advanced to pledge obedience to the new Caliph.

Such an act by Abu 'Ubaidah ﷺ clearly shows us how much he exercised self denial, how much was looking for eternal things and how much he was loyal to the faith he believed in and sacrificed all his treasures to keep high and sublime. He remained a faithful soldier under the rule of Abu Bakr and 'Umar bin Al-Khattab رضي الله عنهما and lived as a humble and poor Muslim. All in all in all he exercised self denial self denial under all conditions.

The Great Commander

During the life of the Prophet ﷺ, he was running all affairs of the state under the guidance of Allâh. All matters related to religion were decided through revelation while worldly things were decided through consultation between the Prophet ﷺ and his Companions.

After the Prophet ﷺ had passed away, revelation ceased and it was now the role of the Muslims to draw on what they had achieved during the life of the Prophet ﷺ. It was, however, a difficult job to be borne by one single person. Therefore, when Abu Bakr ﷺ took over, he began organizing the affairs of the continually broadening state on the basis of sharing powers with his Companions. He appointed Khalid bin Al-Waleed ﷺ as Commander General of the state army, 'Umar ﷺ as the state judge and Abu 'Ubaidah bin Al-Jarrah ﷺ as the treasurer.

It was the time when every effort was needed to help protect the emerging state and when all were for one and one for all. All powers that hid enmity toward Islam had now raised their heads and declared enmity clear and loud.

The Romans were furious to see Islam spreading so quickly and so strongly. Even Arabs in some parts of the Arabian Peninsula found it a good chance to rebel after the death of the Prophet ﷺ.

The Conqueror

Abu 'Ubaidah ﷺ was destined to face all these challenges like any other Muslim loyal to his faith. Hence, he was commissioned by Abu Bakr ﷺ to march to Syria to stop the threats of the Romans forever. Three other armies were also commissioned to the other parts of Syria under the command of 'Amr bin Al-'Aas, Yazid bin Abi Sufyan and Shurahbeel bin Masna ﷺ. All were given instructions that if and when they meet, their General Commander would be Abu 'Ubaidah ﷺ.

The four armies marched to Syria and met together at a place called Al-Yarmouk. Abu 'Ubaidah ﷺ was amazed upon seeing the huge number of soldiers deployed by the Romans. He discussed the problem with his staff and all agreed to inform Abu Bakr ﷺ of the situation and to ask him to dispatch them more soldiers.

More and more Self Denial

Khalid bin Al-Waleed ﷺ was already commissioned by Abu Bakr ﷺ to fight the Persians in the east. To face the huge Roman army, Abu Bakr ﷺ instructed Khalid ﷺ to leave the eastern front and join Abu 'Ubaidah's army. He told him to take over as Commander General of the combined army.

As Khalid ﷺ reached Al-Yarmouk, he informed Abu 'Ubaidah ﷺ of the Caliph's instructions. Abu 'Ubaidah ﷺ immediately obeyed the orders and shared in fighting as an ordinary soldier. His main objective was not to be anything else than a loyal soldier of Islam under the leadership of any other Muslim.

The Muslim army could, through strong belief in the support of Allâh, challenge the Roman army, defeat them and dismiss Hercules out of Syria.

While the battle was hot, a messenger from Al-Madinah came to inform Abu 'Ubaidah ﷺ that Abu Bakr ﷺ had passed away, that 'Umar bin Al-Khattab ﷺ was selected as Caliph and that he had a message from 'Umar ﷺ to him.

The message contained an order from 'Umar to appoint Abu 'Ubaidah ﷺ as Commander General in place of Khalid ﷺ. Abu 'Ubaidah ﷺ read the message and asked the messenger to keep it secret as long as the battle was under the command of Khalid ﷺ.

As the battle ended with a great victory for the Muslims, Abu 'Ubaidah ﷺ informed Khalid ﷺ of the message. Khalid ﷺ read the message, advanced and kissed Abu 'Ubaidah's forehead. He was so influenced by the way Abu 'Ubaidah ﷺ acted. He exclaimed!

"Why did you not tell me before?"

Abu 'Ubaidah ﷺ replied:

"I did not like to confuse you. You know it is not worldly things that we look for. We are all brothers."

Khalid ﷺ accepted the instructions of the Caliph with loyalty and continued his struggle against disbelief under the command of Abu 'Ubaidah ﷺ.

Such an attitude by both men showed how much they were devoted to only one objective; that was, to raise the Word of Allâh high and to spread Islam all over the world.

The Humble Governor

Abu 'Ubaidah ﷺ continued his mission until he, with the Muslim army, spread his control over all of Syria. Hence, 'Umar ﷺ commissioned him to be the Governor of Syria and Commander General of the largest Muslim army. Abu 'Ubaidah ﷺ, however, acted like any other humble soldier of his army. Powers and posts did not make him feel proud over others.

He heard that the people of Damascus admired his morals much and were praising him in their conversations. He feared that he might feel any kind of self-admiration.

Hence, he asked them to gather at one place and addressed them saying:

> "O People, I am a Muslim from the Quraish. Anyone among you, whether white or black, who outweighs me in piety, then he shall be my master."

The poor Governor

'Umar bin Al-Khattab ﷺ, the Caliph, decided to visit Syria. Upon his arrival to Damascus, he asked people to take him to Abu 'Ubaidah's house. He found it a humble house empty of all features of pleasure. He blamed Abu 'Ubaidah ﷺ for being so hard on himself. 'Umar ﷺ asked Abu 'Ubaidah ﷺ to bring him some food. Abu 'Ubaidah ﷺ brought him a basket of some dry and rough bread. 'Umar's tears roll down on his cheeks. He addressed Abu 'Ubaidah ﷺ:

"We all have changed except you."

'Umar ﷺ instructed his treasurer to send Abu 'Ubaidah ﷺ some money. Abu 'Ubaidah ﷺ, however, refused to accept the money and told 'Umar ﷺ:

"I am not working for you. I am working for Allâh's sake. For that I will not accept any worldly compensation."

Abu 'Ubaidah ﷺ lived a poor Governor. He felt the agonies of the poor and the needy and gave them most of his salary. He could not lead a life of pleasure or enjoy any moment of his life while he knew that all he was doing would be calculated either for him or against him on the Day of Judgment.

Preaching Morality

Abu 'Ubaidah ﷺ always advised his Companions to be clean inside as well as outside. Whenever he had a chance to preach to people, he was urging them to be pious and self restrained. Even he was so brave as to advise 'Umar ﷺ himself when he took over rule to shoulder his responsibilities in a good manner and to consult the notable Muslim personalities.

The last commandment he made before he passed away in Jordan was:

"O People, I would like to advise you. If you listen to my advise, you will surely live in peace: Perform prayers, fast Ramadhân, give alms, perform pilgrimage, advise your rulers and do not be misled by worldly things, for if you live one thousand years you will finally end the same as I end now. Allâh has Prescribed death on human beings.

The best among them is the most loyal to his Lord and the most knowledgeable of the Day of Judgment."

The noble Man

Abu 'Ubaidah ﷺ was one of the great Companions of the Prophet ﷺ. He ﷺ himself commended him as the nation's trustworthy of the Muslim *Ummah,* and even he foretold that Abu 'Ubaidah ﷺ would be one of those who would be accepted in Paradise. He was the fighter who spent all his life supporting the message of Islam even under the worst conditions.

'Umar bin Al-Khattab ﷺ admired Abu 'Ubaidah ﷺ so much so that he wished to have thousands like him. 'Amr bin Al-'Aas ﷺ said:

"There are three men from the Quraish, most notable, best in morals and most bashful. They never lie or deny others. They are Abu Bakr, Uthman bin Affan and Abu 'Ubaidah bin Al-Jarrah رضي الله عنهم."

The End of the Journey

As Abu 'Ubaidah ﷺ and his soldiers were marching through Syria and surrounding lands, they were inflicted with plague. 'Umar bin Al- Khattab ﷺ felt sad for Abu 'Ubaidah ﷺ and requested him to come back to Al-Madinah immediately. However, Abu 'Ubaidah ﷺ refused to return to Al-Madinah and told the messenger that he would never escape from the act of Allâh. He also told him that he would never leave his soldiers alone.

He wrote a letter to 'Umar ﷺ saying:

"O Commander of the believers, I know that you need me. However, I am with some Muslim soldiers whom I do not like to leave alone. So, I would like to ask you to leave me with my soldiers."

'Umar ﷺ received the letter and cried much for losing such a great man.

Abu 'Ubaidah ﷺ became very sick and bedridden. He said to those around him:

"Pass my greetings to the Commander of the believers and tell him that I have fulfilled all my obligations as much as I could."

Some days later, Abu 'Ubaidah ﷺ passed away in Jordan. He joined the Prophet ﷺ and his dear Companions in the eternal life.

Abu 'Ubaidah ﷺ started his life in Makkah surrounded with high black mountains. He might have thought before accepting Islam that it would not be possible for him to be a ruler of Syria, but after accepting Islam he built a nation that overtook many parts of the Roman and Persion Empires.

In spite of all the riches that conquests brought to the Muslims, Abu 'Ubaidh ﷺ did not care for such riches or pleasures of life. He continued his life as he originally had been during the life of the Prophet ﷺ.

I would like to tell you about the words said by Mu'az bin Jabl ﷺ, great Companion of the Prophet ﷺ, after Abu 'Ubaidh ﷺ passed away. He said:

> "O people! Ask Allâh to forgive your sins. Anyone of you, who meets Allâh after repentance, Allâh will forgive him. Any one indebted to any other person should settle his debt for every one is encumbered by his debt. Anyone of you not is good terms with his brother should visit him and settle his differences with him. No Muslim should keep in dispute with his brother Muslim more than three days. O Muslims! Today, you have lost a geat man who was most loving, most faithful and most trustworthy, pray for him."

May Allâh bestow his mercy on and bless Abu 'Ubaidah ﷺ for the services he rendered to Islam and the Muslims.

سعد بن أبي وقاص ﵁

-الأسد في عرينه-

Sa'd bin Abi Waqqas ﵁

The Lion in the Den

The First Steps on the Way to Truth

Background

A short time before the advent of Islam, Makkans were mainly interested in satisfying their worldly desires and worshipping idols. They adopted deities which they, in the depth of their hearts, knew that they would not hold them accountable for the evils they were doing. They persisted on enjoying all pleasures because they never thought of a day of reckoning. Every member of each tribe could not imagine anything else other than drawing his sword in defense of his tribal customs and traditions.

The chiefs of Makkah found many means to collect as much money as they could. Their orders were taken for granted and their acts were never questioned. They could, by a single war cry, gather hundreds and thousands to defend the dignity of the tribe. They always invented enemies to use the youth to satisfy their whims.

The youth of Makkah, on the other hand, had nothing to do but to quench their thirst for drinking and women. Young men of rich families were most of the time either chasing after pleasures or preparing for a new invasion against a weaker tribe. However, when they had any leisure time, they only thought of going hunting or drinking.

Sa'd was one of those youth who belonged to a first class family. He was a member of the Quraish tribe, the most dignified tribe in Makkah. He led his life in an atmosphere where no one cared for anything but for personal pleasures and tribal deities.

Roses amid Thorns

However, Sa'd looked with an eye of pity at the youth around him. He was well aware that the trivial pleasures they indulged themselves in were not the ultimate end for which a youth should dedicate his life. Chiefs, slaves and women around him could not convince him that they were doing the right thing. He could, like any other youth, have anything he liked. Those around him were always trying to pull his legs to share with them the short moments of pleasure but he did not like to share in such vanities.

Sa'd was a different man in all respects. He disliked all bad tribal customs and traditions that his people defended. Since the days of early youth, he took another direction. He never shared with his friends their drinking habits. He looked at the idols that his people worshipped with much resentment. He always felt that these stones were not the proper deities to ask for help in difficult times.

Sa'd isolated himself from his fellow tribesmen most of the time. He did not like the bad ways they were following. Rather, he spent many days and nights thinking of the universe and Allâh Alone who created it. He used to go alone in the desert with his eyes fixed on the stars hoping to find a way out of the gloom his people were living. He sat by the window at night listening to the sounds of nature that gave him a sense of communion with the Creator of everything around him. He was always asking himself a question that he could not find an answer to: 'Is it really those idols that control the world?' The moon that shines over earth and the sun that lightens the world would not even accept such an idea. Such idols would not even be able to protect themselves against the scorching sun of the desert.

Finally, he came to the conviction that there must be a greater creator of this universe, who is undoubtedly far more powerful than such idols. He began searching for the creator everywhere. The vast desert, the high mountains, the sky on high with shining stars and the clouds that were racing over him all were signs of a greater and a higher deity. He felt in the depth of his heart that the day to remove all doubt and gloom was close.

There were some people sitting beside the Ka'bah speaking of a man named Muhammad bin Abdullah who was calling people to abandon idols and worship the One Allâh. Sa'd listened to them carefully. They rejected the new faith that came to destroy the legacy of idolatry. He got news that his close friend Abu Bakr ﷺ had followed the new religion. Therefore, he decided to know more about the teachings and principles of the new religion.

As the sun set behind the high mountains of Makkah and all the people went to their homes, Sa'd left to Abu Bakr's house. On the way there, he thought of many questions that he wanted his friend to answer. He was fairly sure that trustworthy Muhammad ﷺ would not falsely claim being Allâh's

Messenger. However, he wanted to be sure of every word he heard about the man and his call.

Islam Introduced to Sa'd

He knocked on the door and was welcomed in by Abu Bakr ﷺ. There, he listened to the clear and pure words of his friend about the new religion. He felt that what he thought of during those nights was correct. He immediately asked his friend to take him to Muhammad ﷺ.

Sa'd felt the opposition that the new religion was facing. He listened to the chiefs of Makkah threatening to inflict severe punishment on those who might follow Muhammad ﷺ. Therefore, he and Abu Bakr ﷺ left under the cover of darkness to where Muhammad ﷺ was preaching to his followers and teaching them the principles of Islam.

As soon as he went inside the room, he heard the Prophet ﷺ reading some Verses of the Noble Qur'ân about the truth of the creation of this world. His heart was filled with satisfaction. Now, he became sure that a new light had come to save his people from the evils they were doing. These were, he thought, the principles and concepts that he was long seeking to adopt. Therefore, he immediately embraced Islam and accepted the change.

Obstinate Mother

Fearing to receive pressure from his family, Sa'd asked his friend Abu Bakr ﷺ to keep his conversion to Islam a secret. He knew that his mother, whom he loved very much, would not easily let him give up the deities of his people and follow the teachings of Muhammad ﷺ.

The new Muslim was secretly meeting the Prophet ﷺ every day to listen to the heavenly Message that was revealed to the Prophet ﷺ. Day after day his faith was becoming stronger and more profound.

The Challenge

One day Sa'd ﷺ came back to his house. There, he saw his mother waiting for him. She angrily asked:

"Is it true that you have become a Muslim?"

Someone had told her that her son had abandoned the religion of his people and followed the new religion. Without any hesitation, he replied:

"Yes, mother! I have followed the light of truth."

He asked her to follow his example and embrace Islam. However, she denied him the right to do so and announced a hunger strike to force him to come back to his old false beliefs.

With all tenderness and mercy, Sa'd ﷺ asked his mother to stop her harassment. He loved her very much and was keen not to make her suffer. She insisted and told him that she would not eat or drink till she died or he would go back to the religion of his forefathers.

At the end of the first day, the old woman became very weak. Sa'd ﷺ was suffering a great conflict of whether to hold on to his faith or to please his mother. She was very decisive and did not accept any appeal.

The second day, the old woman began fainting and she was about to die. Sa'd ﷺ looked at her with tears in his eyes and said:

"O mother, listen to me! If you have one hundred souls and you lose them one after the other to make me abandon this religion, I would not do it. I have found my way to happiness in this life and in the Hereafter."

His words touched her heart. She thought that his acceptance of Islam was a mere desire that he would quit for her sake. When she knew that her son was serious, she stopped her hunger strike.

The Prophet ﷺ knew of the story and praised Sa'd's steadfastness. Verses of the Noble Qur'ân were revealed unto the Prophet ﷺ commenting on the events:

"But if they (both) strive with you to make you join in worship with Me others that of which you have no knowledge, then obey them not; but behave with them in the world kindly." (31:15)

Through this trial, Sa'd ﷺ became stronger and more enlightened. He was being prepared for greater trials that would perfect his attitudes and feelings. He proved that a believer would not exchange his belief for the whole world.

Defending the Faith

The Muslims suffered hard times at the beginning of the Islamic call. Slaves who found their salvation in Islam and poor and weak families who hoped to find justice in Islam were tortured. Some of them were even killed by pagans.

Sa'd ﷺ himself suffered much injustice from his family. He was from a noble family who could provide protection for him against others but he did not feel at ease to see his fellow

Muslims receive all these types of torture. Therefore, he tried his best to save them from the agonies that the Quraish inflicted on them.

He continued his life in Makkah under such harsh conditions. He spent three years of hunger and suffering with the Prophet ﷺ at Abi Tâlib's valley where the pagans confined the Muslims under the scorching sun of the desert. In spite of all this, he never showed any signs of weakness or surrender.

The Emigrant

Days were passing very heavy on the new Muslims in Makkah. The chiefs of Makkah were sparing no effort to make them recant. Most of the early Muslims were slaves and weak persons who had no tribes to support them. Even those who belonged to the Quraish tribe received their share of torture and oppression. The pagans did their best to make the few number of Muslims abandon their new faith. The Prophet ﷺ himself was treated very badly by his uncle Abu Lahab, and his uncle's wife Umm Jameel.

Hardships Test for True Believers

The Prophet ﷺ and his Companions felt that if they continued to stay in Makkah, they would not be able to spread or even to maintain their faith. The pagans were plotting day and night to keep the new faith limited to the first few Muslims who embraced Islam during these thirteen years of struggle. They even plotted to kill the Prophet ﷺ on the day he migrated to Al-Madinah.

Therefore, the Prophet ﷺ decided to allow his Companions to migrate to Al-Madinah (formerly Yathrib) after he had made an agreement with the inhabitants of the town to protect him and his followers.

Many Muslims left their properties and houses to be robbed

by the pagans and emigrated to Al-Madinah to save their lives and faith. Some of them, like Suhaib ﷺ, surrendered all of their wealth to the pagans in order to escape the humiliation and pressures imposed on them by the pagans.

The March to the New Land

Under the cover of a dark night, Sa'd ﷺ left his house and took a road different from the usual roads to escape from the eyes of the guards whom the Quraish had assigned to stop the Muslims from leaving Makkah.

At the outskirts of the city, he looked behind with sorrow and tear-filled eyes. He never wanted to leave the city where he was brought up. However, there was no other choice. He felt that in order to maintain his Faith, he had to abandon everything he liked in his city.

After a short while, he turned his camel's face towards Al-Madinah and marched in a very long journey to the new Islamic State. He thought that he had not been the only person to leave his family, house and homeland. So many times he heard the Prophet ﷺ telling of persons who sacrificed all worldly things to maintain their beliefs. The camel was going slowly through the vast desert over dunes of sand and rocky roads and the lone young man was, with every step ahead, contemplating the new life he was going to live in the new land.

Ten long days passed. Sa'd ﷺ was about to reach Al-Madinah. At the first house of the town, he felt safe and secure. Many persons met him asking him to be their guest. He never thought that he would receive such a warm welcome. Eventually, he was sure that it was Islam which made these people so kind. The man whom he took as a brother, asked him to share his property till he was able to have his own.

Islam had already spread in Al-Madinah. Most people there were ready to put everything they had under the disposal of the newcomers. All men and women were impatiently waiting for the arrival of the leader to build the Islamic State under Allâh's Guidance.

Finally, two camels behind the mirage of the desert were moving slowly on the glowing sand. All the people of Al-Madinah went to where the small caravan was approaching. As the people of Al-Madinah were sure that the Prophet ﷺ and his Companion, Abu Bakr ؓ, had arrived, they received them with a very pleasant chant:

"The full moon has risen from behind the hills.
All praise is due to Allâh whenever a preacher calls to the way of Allâh."

The New Islamic State

Sa'd ؓ was very happy to see the Prophet ﷺ and his best friend Abu Bakr ؓ again. When he hugged the Prophet ﷺ and Abu Bakr ؓ, he felt inside that a new stage of struggle had now begun. All the Muslims started building the first mosque on the earth. For the long time, they were not free to worship Allâh openly. They actively participated in building the symbol of Islam.

Sa'd ؓ and his fellow Muslims began applying the teachings of Islam to all aspects of their lives. The Prophet ﷺ and his Companions were now up to a new challenge.

★★★

The Sincere Believer

Many times did the Prophet ﷺ tell Sa'd ﷺ:

"You are the supporter of Islam wherever you are."

Thus, Sa'd ﷺ took these words as an objective second to none. From then on, he made those words as true as he could.

As soon as the Prophet ﷺ established the pillars of the new state, he began sending groups of the Muslims to the tribes around Al-Madinah to call them to Islam. At the same time, Muslims began preparing themselves to encounter new challenges. Several armed squads were commissioned to control the ways followed by the Quraish caravans on the trade routes to Yemen and Damascus.

The First Battle of Islam

Sa'd ﷺ was fully prepared to participate in any effort to spread the light of Islam and to show Makkans the power the Muslims had attained. A squad of sixty men was commissioned by the Prophet ﷺ to tour the desert looking for any sign of challenge. Sa'd ﷺ with his fellow Muslims once came face to face with the pagans at some place in the desert. No fighting took place but Sa'd ﷺ wanted to show the enemy a sign of strength and freedom. He shot an arrow toward them and hence he was the first Muslim to start the endless battle between believers and disbelievers.

In the second year after emigration to Al-Madinah, Muslims

began patrolling outside Al-Madinah for security purposes. They received the news of a Quraish caravan nearby. They went towards it to check it but Abu Sufyan knew of the plan and changed his way. Hence, the caravan escaped the ambush.

However, the pagans felt the danger and wanted to stop the source of such threat to their trade and whole existence. They shouted the cry of war and gathered one thousand fighters to attack the Muslims. The Muslims, on the other hand, could barely collect three hundred poorly equipped men to defend their Faith and State.

Both armies met at a place called Badr and the battle started. Sa'd ﷺ and the other Muslims fought a very fierce battle and within a short time gave a very serious blow to the pagans.

Steadfast as Ever

The pagans were very angry for the loss they received at the hands of the Muslims. Therefore, they gathered three thousand warriors the next year and marched toward Al-Madinah to revenge themselves against the Muslims. Both armies met near Mount Uhud. The Prophet ﷺ deployed some fifty archers on the mountain to foil any attack from behind by the pagans. He instructed them not to leave their positions whatever the result of the battle was. In the beginning of the fight, the Muslims won the battle. The archers saw the pagans fleeing the battlefield. Therefore, they left their positions and began collecting war booty. The pagan horsemen found it a good chance to attack the Muslims from behind. After a while, the battle turned into a heavy loss for the Muslims. Many Muslim soldiers left the battlefield and headed toward Al-Madinah. They thought that the Prophet ﷺ was killed. However, a few Muslim soldiers held to their positions and fought bravely to the last minute of their lives. Sa'd ﷺ was one of those who kept fighting. He took a position in front of the Prophet ﷺ and began shooting arrows at the pagans. At this difficult time, he heard the sweetest words from the Prophet ﷺ:

> "Sa'd! shoot them, may my father and mother be sacrificed for you."

He was receiving every pagan soldier with his bare chest to protect the Prophet ﷺ and hence he received many blows. However, he did not feel any pain for he was defending the Messenger of Allâh.

Sa'd ﷺ participated in all other battles that took place between the Muslims and the pagans. He proved to be a true believer in the face of the enemies of Islam. He did not spare one minute of his time to firmly establish the Word of Allâh all over the Arabian Peninsula.

Whenever the Prophet ﷺ met Sa'd ﷺ, he said some nice words to him that made him very happy. The words were that he would not exchange for the whole world:

> "This is my uncle. Would anyone of you show me his uncle?"

The Merciful Conqueror

Eight years had now passed since the Muslims built their state in Al-Madinah. Islam became very strong and the Muslims were preparing to conquer Makkah. Makkans had already breached the terms agreed to with the Muslims to stop fighting for ten years.

They attacked a Muslim tribe and killed some of its members. Sa'd ﷺ felt very happy that he would see his homeland again.

He had many times tried with other migrants to enter Makkah peacefully to visit the Ka'bah, but the pagans prevented them from realizing this wish. Now it was time to see his beloved city.

The Muslims marched to Makkah. Sa'd ﷺ looked at the marching army behind and felt inside that the Word of Allâh would never be foiled. The Muslims entered Makkah peacefully without facing any resistance. Sa'd ﷺ immediately went to the Ka'bah and listened to the words *Allâhu Akbar* (Allâh is the Greatest) announced loud and clear at the same place where he had first been hiding for fear that the pagans might humiliate him.

The Farewell Pilgrimage

Immediately after conquering Makkah, the Prophet ﷺ ordered his Companions to prepare for pilgrimage. Before conquering Makkah, the Prophet ﷺ and his Companions tried to visit the Ka'bah but the pagans prevented them from entering Makkah. Now they were free to practice the rites of Islam as they liked.

Sa'd ﷺ stood with the Prophet ﷺ and the other Muslims at Mount 'Arafat. There they prayed to Allâh and thanked Him for the blessings he gave to them. On the day of 10th Dhul-Hijjah the Prophet ﷺ gathered all the Muslims at Mina and preached to them the last revelation from Allâh. Sa'd ﷺ listened carefully to the last Verses of the Noble Qur'ân:

"This day, I have perfected your religion for you,

completed My Favor upon you, and have chosen for you Islâm as your religion." (5:3)

Sa'd ﷺ and many other Companions of the Prophet ﷺ knew that this Verse meant that the mission of the Prophet ﷺ had been completed and that he would leave them soon.

The Prophet ﷺ Passes Away

A short period after completing the pilgrimage, Sa'd ﷺ received a heavy shock which left him heart broken to the end of his life. They said that the Prophet ﷺ had passed away. For a while he did not believe it, but later on, with tears running down his cheeks, he shared in burying the example of tenderness and mercy. Yes! The Prophet ﷺ had passed away.

The Conqueror

Sa'd had been taught by the Prophet that spreading the Word of Allâh should not stop at any time or at any place. It is the Eternal Message that should prevail all over the world.

Abu Bakr was selected as the Caliph. As Islam was not deeply rooted in some parts of Arabia, many of the people in these parts reverted to idolatry as soon as they received the news of the death of the Prophet. Some Arab chiefs found it a good chance to regain their privileges over others, which they had lost after the advent of Islam. However, Abu Bakr supported by Sa'd and other true Muslims, vowed to conquer the rebels and restore peace to the Arabian Peninsula. Sa'd fought as a sincere soldier against the apostates. He and the other true Muslims finally defeated the powers of evil and undermined any attempts to return to idolatry in the Arabian Peninsula.

Before Abu Bakr passed away, he proposed to hand over the trust to 'Umar bin Al-Khattab. At that period of time, the Muslims began sending their armies outside of the borders of the Arabian Peninsula to call other nations to Islam.

In continuation of Abu Bakr's efforts to stop any threat against the Islamic State, 'Umar thought that the Persians, who first rejected to hear the Word of Allâh and prepared to fight the Muslims, should not be given the chance to threaten Islam. Therefore, he decided to take the initiative. Al-Muthana bin Harithah ﷺ asked 'Umar ﷺ to fight the Persians in order to stop their attacks at the borders of the Islamic State. He told 'Umar ﷺ that it was a good time to defeat the Persians for they were suffering some conflicts over power. 'Umar ﷺ welcomed the idea and wished to lead the army to Persia himself. However, the Muslims objected to the idea and suggested trusting the mission to another leader. After a lengthy discussion, all the Muslims agreed to Sa'd bin Abi Waqqas ﷺ. 'Umar ﷺ immediately shouted:

"Yes, you are true, it should be Sa'd ﷺ, for he is the lion in the den."

A Leader with an Honorable Mission

'Umar ﷺ called Sa'd ﷺ and told him that all the Muslims had agreed to appoint him as the commander of the army. Sa'd ﷺ accepted the mission and began preparing for the march.

As soon as the army was ready to march to Iraq, 'Umar ﷺ stood in front of the army and gave the commander the last advice:

"Sa'd! I order you to fight the Persians. Listen to me and hold fast to my words. You are going to face a very hard obstacle that you cannot overcome unless you observe truth and goodness. You should know that every battle should be prepared for by having good equipment, let your equipment be patience. Do not be deceived by saying to yourself:

'I am the Prophet's uncle,'

for there is no kinship dear to Allâh except loyalty to his teachings."

Sa'd listened carefully to the words of the Caliph and promised to do his best to stick to the advice. He felt a shiver go through his body when 'Umar instructed him to strictly observe the teachings of the Prophet.

Sa'd led an army of thirty thousand soldiers to a place called Al-Qadisiyah in Iraq. There he saw the Persians deploying their army under the leadership of Rustam.

As soon as he arrived to Al-Qadisiyah, he sent a letter to 'Umar informing him of the situation on field and waiting for orders to start the battle. 'Umar replied by a letter that could be considered the most honorable law of combat that history ever recorded. 'Umar wrote to Sa'd saying:

"I order you and your soldiers to fear Allâh at all times, for fearing Allâh is the best weapon you have against your enemy. I order you and your soldiers to guard against evil deeds as much as you guard against your enemy. Evil deeds are more dangerous to your army than your enemy is. You will win because your enemy is a disbeliever. Ask Allâh to help you overcome your desires as much as you ask Him to help you overcome your enemy. Do not force the Muslims to march when they are tired and keep them ready with full strength to meet the enemy. Take rest one day every week to keep your army fully ready. Do not come near any village inhabited by our protected peaceful allies and do not allow anyone of your soldiers to enter any village unless you are sure he will act properly.

Look out scouting is the best way to know the power of your enemy. Therefore, give such a mission to whom you best trust and provide them with the best horses."

Exchange of letters continued between the Caliph and the commander. They were exchanging information and drawing plans to achieve victory. One month passed while Sa'd ﷺ was waiting for the deadline to attack. He spent all this period studying the battlefield and preparing for the final cry of war.

Islam had taught Sa'd ﷺ and all Muslims not to fight any nation before calling them to Islam. Therefore, Sa'd ﷺ sent messengers to Yazdajurd, the Persian King, calling him to embrace Islam, to pay tribute or, if he rejected both options, to fight.

The first delegation called the King to accept Islam. They explained to him the principles and concepts of Islam. Instead of accepting this kind call, the King began blaming the Muslims for coming to his land and threatened to undermine their religion. The Muslim delegation told him of the evils they were doing before they became Muslims. They finally told him that he was free to choose either to accept the religion of Islam, to pay tribute or to face definite defeat.

The King showed the delegation much humiliation and anger. He asked his soldiers to fill sacks of soil and force the members of the delegation to carry them on their backs till they leave the city. He told them that he would send Rustam to bury their leader and the Muslim army in the Qadisiyah trench.

When Rustam knew how the King acted, he felt very troubled. He foresaw a sign of defeat in the soil carried by the delegation to the Muslim leader.

Negotiating a Peaceful Solution

Rustam asked Sa'd to send him another messenger to negotiate. Al-Mugheerah bin Shu'bah came to Rustam. As soon as he arrived, Rustam started negotiating with him in a very gentle manner and asked him to tell Sa'd that it was better for them to leave to their homeland. Al-Mugheerah told Rustam that it was their mission to spread the light of Islam. He explained to him the principles of Islam. Rustam felt the just teachings of Islam and asked the messenger to give him time to discuss them with the heads of the nation. Rustam told his people that it was better for them to accept Islam, but they refused.

Sa'd sent the third messenger, Rab'i bin 'Amer to Rustam. Before his arrival to the place of the Persian army, the Persians wanted to show him how rich and powerful they were. The whole palace was furnished with gold and silver. Rab'i came inside on his horse with his humble dress until he stepped on the carpets. The soldiers asked him to leave his horse out and to put down his arms. He refused and stepped ahead on the carpets and ruined them with his spear. He jumped down from the back of his horse and sat beside Rustam. He was not amazed by the vanity they wanted to show him.

Rustam inquired about the Muslims' motives behind coming to his land. Rab'i told him that they were ordered by Allâh to spread the true word of Islam over the whole earth. Rustam asked him whether he was a chief. The humble messenger replied that the Muslims were like one body and anyone of them would decide for others.

Rustam told Sa'd ﷺ that he would give the Muslims a bitter defeat if they insisted on fighting.

Both armies began preparing for the battle. The Persians prepared about one hundred thousand fully armed soldiers supported by elephants and other heavy combat equipment. The Muslims on the opposite side gathered with their humble arms to fight against this huge army. Sa'd ﷺ directed his soldiers saying:

> "Obey the orders of Khalid ﷺ, for he is conveying my orders to you. Be sure that you will win if you favour to die for the sake of Allâh. You are promised by Him to take this land."

Sa'd ﷺ spent the whole day giving the army a spirit of sacrifice and courage.

The timing of operation was initiated by the words *Allâhu Akbar* (Allâh is the Greatest). The Muslim army faced a sudden shock. Their horses did not move forward for fear of the advancing elephants that the Persians put in the first line. However, some of the Muslim archers began shooting at the elephants. They forced the elephants to turn back in terror and throw off their riders. The whole day, the Muslims fought a very fierce battle but the positions of both armies did not change.

The second day a new round of fighting started. The Muslims received support by an army led by Hashim bin 'Utbah coming from Damascus.

The battle continued and the Muslims were sacrificing their souls to raise the Islamic banner high. The fighting went on all the night. When the sun rose, it was clear that the Muslims had the upper hand. Rustam tried to escape but he was finally killed.

The Reward

This was the life of our hero who sacrificed all his life for the service of Islam. He faced the pagans in Makkah, migrated to Al-Madinah and fought several battles to spread the light of the Noble Qur'ân.

During his days of old age, he sincerely hoped to meet his Lord light and free from all burdens. He kept praying and exercising strict observance of Allâh's teachings. Although the Prophet ﷺ told him that he would dwell in Paradise, he was spending all his time praying to Allâh to forgive his sins.

One night with a clear sky and shining moon, the hero lied down on a humble bed. His son was sitting beside his head crying. Sa'd ﷺ said:

"Do not cry my son. Don't you know that your father was promised Paradise?"

He closed his eyes with a pleasant smile on his face and the small and weak body became cold.

طلحة بن عبيد الله رضي الله عنه

– الشهيد الحي –

Talhah bin 'Ubaidullah رضي الله عنه

The Alive Martyr

On the Way to Truth

The sun was about to set behind the high mountains of Makkah and the whole universe was shrouded with serenity. Darkness soon covered the city and no more sounds were heard on those high mountains surrounding the city.

A group of young men walked along the side of the road outside of Makkah and began chatting. Their voices sometimes became louder and with every word, they were warning each other of the spies of the Board of Governors of Makkah. They were sure that any word heard by those chiefs would mean a harsh punishment.

They kept silent for a while to listen to the far songs of trade caravans heading to Makkah. There, under the scarf of darkness, a caravan was slowly coming closer on the way back from Syria. To their surprise, a young man stepped down from his camel and ran toward the group.

The young men looked at each other, and to their surprise, they saw Talhah bin 'Ubaidullah coming to greet them. He hastily asked whether they had any news from Makkah.

Az-Zubair bin Al-Awwam ﷺ told the young man that the city was in turmoil. He added that the trustworthy Muhammad ﷺ had been sent by Allâh to preach a new religion, calling people to abandon worship of stone idols and to direct their faces and prayers to the One Allâh, Who created them and everything around them. Muhammad ﷺ told them to be kind to their slaves and to stop fighting each other. These words touched the sense of charity which Talhah felt better than many others. Az-Zubair ﷺ told him that the new Prophet ﷺ urged the rich to be kind to their fellow poor men. Talhah immediately inquired whether anyone of the Quraish tribe believed in him. Az-Zubair ﷺ replied that Abu Bakr ﷺ had believed in and supported him. The young man asked with zeal:

"What about you?"

Az-Zubair ﷺ replied:

"We all believe in him and follow him."

Talhah looked at the faces of the young men. From the first instance, he discovered that they were the best young men he knew in Makkah. He directly vowed that he would follow Muhammad ﷺ and defend the Message he brought from Allâh. He told the group that the man was a true Messenger from Allâh.

The group of young men was surprised how Talhah knew this fact. Talhah felt the effect of that strange question on their faces and immediately asked them to meet him at Abu Bakr's house to give them full account of his journey to Syria.

The young men hurried to Abu Bakr's house. Az-Zubair ﷺ told Abu Bakr ﷺ about the events and asked him to allow Talhah in to hear news from him. The young men were very anxious to listen to Talhah.

As soon as Talhah arrived home, he left his camels with loads still on and hurried to Abu Bakr's house. There he found the men waiting to hear his story. Talhah did not like to keep them waiting long. So, he immediately started telling them what he saw and heard while in Syria. He said:

> "While I was at Busra market, I heard a monk inquiring whether there were any traders from Makkah. I hurried to him and said, 'Yes, I am from Makkah.' The monk then asked me: 'Had Ahmad (another name of the Prophet ﷺ) appeared?' I inquired who could be Ahmad? He said: 'Son of Abdullah son of Abdul Muttalib. He should appear this month. He is the last Prophet and he will appear in Makkah and emigrate to a land full of palm trees. Be the first to believe in him if you can.' Now you see why I stopped my journey and came back. Would you please take me to the Prophet ﷺ!"

Abu Bakr ﷺ and the other young men felt very happy to hear this news. This was the second young man from Taim clan to accept Islam. Abu Bakr ﷺ took Talhah to the Prophet ﷺ and there Talhah embraced Islam and told the Prophet ﷺ of the monk's glad tidings.

However, Talhah ﷺ was told to keep his belief in Islam secret, or he would face heavy oppression by the chiefs of Makkah. Abu Bakr ﷺ told him how much pressure the new Muslims had been subjected to because they believed in the new message. Hence, the man kept the story of embracing Islam secret. He continued his life unhindered by the chiefs of Makkah. He went on trading and helping the Muslims and providing them with financial resources.

Even after it had been known that Talhah ﷺ embraced Islam, the chiefs of Makkah could not cause him any harm due to his financial strength. As usual, they were respecting money more than anything else. Because of his free trading movement, Talhah ﷺ came in contact with many Jews and Christians. Most of the people of the Bible knew that it was the time for a new Prophet to appear. Most historians confirmed that Talhah was a believer even before the advent of Islam as the names of his sons: Muhammad, Imran, Jesus, Moses, Ishmael and Isaac denote.

The Emigrant

All Arabs and even other nations knew that a new Prophet ﷺ had been sent to call people to abandon idols and worship the only true Allâh. However, the situation in Makkah was very hard for the Prophet ﷺ and other Muslims. The Prophet ﷺ spent thirteen years calling to Islam but few people, mostly weak men and slaves, believed in the message he proclaimed. The Quraish chiefs did their best to prevent any contact between the Prophet ﷺ and members of tribes who visited Makkah for pilgrimage or trading. They kept him under strict control and assigned several men to follow his steps. The Muslims, on the other hand, were constantly subjected to cruelties and oppression to make them abstain from spreading the call of Islam.

The Prophet ﷺ, filled with sorrow for the conditions of his followers, told them to seek refuge at places other than Makkah. In spite of the strong siege the Makkans made around him, he secretly concluded a pledge of protection with some chiefs of Yathrib (A city about 400 kilometers away from Makkah).

The pledge gave the Prophet ﷺ and his Companions the chance to escape the torture of the Quraish and to freely preach Islam. Hence, the Prophet ﷺ instructed his Companions to emigrate to that town where they would find help and safety.

The Muslims left Makkah to Yathrib (later named by the

Prophet ﷺ as Al-Madinah) where their brothers in Islam *Al-Ansâr* (the supporters) were waiting to welcome every emigrant. They left the land where they had suffered much humiliation and agonies. None of them, including the Prophet ﷺ, wanted to depart but there was no other way out to avoid oppression. However, they were sure that if a tent was blown away by wind, a palace was going to be created in its place. High winds could never blemish the face of the sun.

They left to a society where love and brotherhood ruled. It was the society within which they were going to build their new state of truth and pure belief in Allâh. The Noble Qur'ân tells us about the emigrants:

> "And those who, before them, had homes (in Al-Madinah) and had adopted the Faith, love those who emigrate to them, and have no jealousy in their breasts for that which they have been given (from the booty of Banû An-Nadîr), and give them (emigrants) preference over themselves even though they were in need of that. And whosoever is saved from his own covetousness such are they who will be the successful." (59:9)

All the Muslims, individuals and groups, secretly left Makkah, but the Prophet ﷺ, Abu Bakr and 'Ali رضي الله عنهما remained there to be sure that no other Muslims would be left behind. On a very dark night, the Prophet ﷺ and Abu Bakr ﷺ left to Al-Madinah to join their companions and start a new stage of struggle for the proclamation of the Word of Allâh.

The Prophet ﷺ stood with his Companion, Abu Bakr ﷺ, outside of Makkah, looked back in sorrow with tears going down his cheeks and said addressing Makkah:

"Allâh knows that you are the dearest city to my heart. Had your people not expelled me, I would not have left you."

Talhah ﷺ was always traveling outside of Makkah. He was outside of Makkah when the Prophet ﷺ and Abu Bakr ﷺ emigrated to Al-Madinah. He was passing near Al-Madinah on his way back from Syria with a trade caravan. He saw all the inhabitants of the town camping outside of Al-Madinah. He knew that it was not a festival time. He inquired about the event and was told that the inhabitants of the town were waiting for the arrival of the Prophet ﷺ.

Talhah ﷺ immediately left to Makkah to meet the Prophet ﷺ on the way before his arrival to Al-Madinah. At a place near Al-Madinah, he met them. He told the Prophet ﷺ how anxious the people of Al-Madinah were to meet him. He gave the Prophet ﷺ and Abu Bakr ﷺ new clothes for their entry to Al-Madinah and continued his trip to Makkah.

Talhah ﷺ resumed his voyage to Makkah because he brought with him goods from Syria for some merchants in Makkah. Upon arriving in Makkah, Talhah ﷺ delivered all the goods in his custody to the people for whom he brought them and left the city with his family under the cover of darkness to Al-Madinah.

Upon arriving in Al-Madinah, Talhah ﷺ went to the Prophet ﷺ in the newly-built mosque and offered to help in any way possible. He was a sincere Companion of the Prophet ﷺ. He kept going to the new mosque built by the Muslims to listen to the teachings of the Prophet ﷺ and share in building the new

Islamic State. He sacrificed all he had for the sake of Islam and did his best to spread the message of Islam.

The first battle of Islam

When the Muslims emigrated from Makkah, they left behind their wealth and houses which the pagans robbed in day light.

As Talhah ﷺ had good experience of roads that trade caravans follow to Syria and Yemen, he was instructed by the Prophet ﷺ to look for the Quraish caravan bound to Makkah from Syria. Both Talhah ﷺ and Saeed bin Zaid رضي الله عنهما were prepared to carry out the mission. They kept waiting until they saw the caravan coming from Syria.

However, the Prophet ﷺ had already received news about the caravan and went on to capture it. Talhah ﷺ arrived in Al-Madinah to discover that the Prophet ﷺ had left Al-Madinah. The Quraish knew of the Muslims' plan to catch the caravan. Therefore, they gathered an army of one thousand fighters to rescue the caravan.

In spite of the fact that Abu Sufyan, the caravan leader, changed his way and escaped the capture of the Muslims, the Quraish army insisted on fighting the Muslims to eradicate the message of Islam and the threat of Muslims forever. They marched with arrogance to Badr to meet the Muslim army.

Both armies fought a big battle. Although the Muslim army was only one third of the pagan army, they, by the Help of Allâh and their sincere devotion, defeated the pagan army. Seventy pagan soldiers, including several chiefs, were killed and another seventy soldiers were taken as prisoners of war by the Muslims.

Talhah ﷺ felt very sad to lose the chance of fighting the powers of evil. He could not share in this battle. Even though he kept waiting at Al-Madinah, the Prophet ﷺ, after coming back victorious, gave him a share of the booty and considered him as if he had participated in the battle.

Uhud Battle - Talhah's Day

In the third year after emigration to Al-Madinah, the Quraish gathered a huge army to avenge the loss they had at Badr Battle. They had lost the first major battle against the Muslims. They did not accept the result of battle. The chiefs of Makkah asked Abu Sufyan to allocate the funds he had from the caravan that escaped the capture of the Muslims for the coming battle.

Three thousand fighters with their allies marched toward Al-Madinah to revenge themselves on the Muslims. Some women also marched with the army to support and encourage the fighters.

The Prophet ﷺ received news of the army gathered by the Quraish to undermine the call of Islam. He discussed with his Companions about the best plan to face the huge Quraish army. Most of them, with the support of the Prophet ﷺ agreed to stay inside the borders of Al-Madinah to defend the city against the attacking army. However, some zealous young men asked the Prophet ﷺ to meet the Quraish army outside of Al-Madinah. They thought that the Quraish would think that the Muslims feared to meet their army in an open battle. The Prophet ﷺ positively responded to their wish. The Muslim army marched toward Uhud Mount to meet the pagan army. On the way there, some Hypocrites objected to the plan to fight an open battle and cowardly left back to Al-Madinah before meeting the Quraish army. Hence, the Muslim army lost a third of its number, but the devoted Muslims continued their march to the battlefield.

Shortly after reaching the site of the battle, the Prophet ﷺ deployed his men in their positions. He selected fifty archers and positioned them on a small hill to protect the backs of the Muslim army. He urged them to stick to their positions whatever the result of the battle might be. Fighting started fiercely and from the very beginning it was clear that the Muslims were winning the battle. The pagan army began retreating in spite of all the encouragement they received from their women behind them. They left the battle scene toward Makkah and suffered a big blow. Upon seeing the pagans retreating and the Muslims collecting booty, the Muslim archers insisted, against the advice of their leader, on leaving their positions and sharing in the collection of the booty. Khalid bin Al-Waleed, the leader of the pagan horsemen, was eagerly waiting for this chance. He turned around the hill, killed the few archers who remained on the hill and attacked the Muslim army from behind. The balance of the battle changed in favour of the pagans.

Talhah ﷺ Sacrifices Himself for the Prophet ﷺ

On that day, which was rightfully called "Talhah's day", the Prophet ﷺ with few of his Companions kept steadfast to their positions and fought a fierce battle. Many of the Muslim fighters heard news that the Prophet ﷺ was killed. Hence, they left the battle scene to Al-Madinah. The Prophet ﷺ suffered severe injuries in his face. Talhah ﷺ, kept very close to the Prophet ﷺ and decided to protect him against those who wanted to kill him. He received so many blows until his body became red with blood. His right hand was struck by so many arrows that it was paralyzed by the injuries it received. However, the brave and sincere soldier saved the life of the Prophet ﷺ. He carried the Prophet ﷺ on his back and hid him behind a huge rock. He sacrificed his soul for the sake of the Prophet ﷺ.

The battle ended, but Talhah's body was profusely bleeding. The Prophet ﷺ saw the condition of Talhah ﷺ and told his Companions:

"If you wish to see a martyr walking among you, look at Talhah." (*At-Tirmidhi*)

Abu Bakr, ﷺ recalling that day, said:

"It was really Talhah's day. He did his best to protect the Prophet ﷺ when other Muslim soldiers escaped the battlefield."

On that day, the Prophet ﷺ told his followers that Talhah ﷺ deserved Paradise for his faithfulness and sincerity to his faith.

Talhah ﷺ kept at home for several days until his wounds healed. He was now and then visited by the Prophet ﷺ. The Prophet ﷺ praised his steadfastness in the battle and foretold to him that he would enter Paradise for his devotion.

The battle of Trench

The pagans thought that the Muslims had become too weak to withstand another battle. The chiefs of the Quraish urged the other tribes of Arabia to share in their final battle against the Muslims. The Jews, on the other hand, urged the Arabs to attack the Muslims while they were weak. They felt jealous to see Islam spreading among the people of Al-Madinah so quickly. Moreover, they had lost their control over the people of Al-

Madinah due to Islam.

The allies gathered an army of ten thousand soldiers and headed to Al-Madinah to destroy Islam forever. They were heavily armed and well prepared for the battle.

The Muslims were not strong enough to fight such a huge army. The Prophet ﷺ and his Companions discussed the best way to avoid being crushed by the allies. Some Companions of the Prophet ﷺ suggested to fight an open battle, for they were sure that Allâh would help them against their enemy. Some other Companions thought it would be better to keep inside Al-Madinah to defend it against the aggressors. The Prophet ﷺ listened carefully to these suggestions, but found that none of them would help to defeat the attackers.

Salman Al-Farisi ﷺ told the Prophet ﷺ that his people in Persia used to build huge fortresses or dig wide trenches around their cities when they were attacked by their enemies. Hence, he suggested to dig a wide trench at the weak points of Al-Madinah and to deploy soldiers behind the trench to stop trespassers. The Prophet ﷺ and his Companions welcomed this suggestion. They all shared in digging the trench. Talhah ﷺ did his best to complete digging the trench before the arrival of the enemy.

To their great surprise, the pagans arrived near Al-Madinah to find it surrounded with a wide trench. They had not seen such a military trick before. Many of them tried to cross over the trench, but they were killed by the Muslim soldiers who were positioned at the other side of the trench.

Back to Makkah with Humiliation

The weather was very cold. Talhah ﷺ spent several nights

guarding one point of the trench to prevent the enemy from breaking through his side. He killed several enemy soldiers who tried to cross over the trench.

After one month of hard siege around the city, the pagans felt that they would not be able to overcome the Muslims. A high cold wind, sent by Allâh, blew through their tents and disrupted their positions.

Punishment of the Traitors

The Jews, who had promised the pagans to help them in their fighting against the Muslims, were warned by a Muslim that the Quraish were leaving their positions and retreating back to their home. They would leave them alone with the Muslims who would kill all of them for their treachery against the Muslims. They were suggested that they should ask the pagans to surrender some of their chiefs to them to be sure that they would not leave them at the mercy of the Muslims. However, the pagans refused this request and left back to Makkah.

The Jews broke all the promises they gave to the Muslims to support them in their battles against their enemies. Talhah ﷺ and the other Muslims were very eager to punish the traitors. They marched with the Prophet ﷺ to the place of Bani Quraitha and surrounded their homes.

The Jews surrendered to the Muslims. Their men were killed and their children and women were taken as slaves. It was a just punishment for the traitors who plotted to destroy Islam.

The Conquest of Makkah

The Muslims' Attempt to Perform '*Umrah*

The Prophet ﷺ instructed his Companions that he wished to visit Makkah to perform a '*Umrah*. He asked them to prepare for the trip. He also told them that they should march unarmed, for the trip was peaceful. He did not like any confrontation with the pagans.

Upon arriving at a place called Hudaibiyah, the Muslims found that the pagans had sent some horsemen to prevent the Muslims from entering Makkah. The horsemen tried several times to provoke the Muslims; however, the Muslims did not react.

The chiefs of the Quraish requested the Prophet ﷺ to enter into negotiations to settle the differences between the two parties. The Prophet ﷺ responded positively. Hence, both parties agreed to have a truce for ten years and the Muslims to go back to Al-Madinah and to come back to visit the Ka'bah the following year.

Some of the Muslims were not satisfied with the agreement. However, they knew later on that it was in favour of the Muslims. The Prophet ﷺ now had time to call other tribes of Arabia to Islam without any objection by the Quraish. Many tribes accepted Islam which added to the strength of the Muslims.

As usual, the pagans did not respect the agreement. Some

allies of the Quraish attacked the allies of the Muslims and killed some of them. The chiefs of the Quraish were aware of the big mistake they had committed. Hence, they sent Abu Sufyan to Al-Madinah to negotiate another agreement with the Prophet ﷺ. However, the Prophet ﷺ did not accept Abu Sufyan's excuses. It was a good chance for the Muslims, who had become very strong, to continue their message and destroy the center of idolatry forever.

The Prophet ﷺ gave instructions to his Companions to march to conquer Makkah.

All Muslims, both emigrants and supporters, were keen to put an end to the continued threats by the Makkans. All Muslims from around the Arabian Peninsula gathered at Al-Madinah to share in this mission. In the eighth year after emigration, the Muslim army marched toward Makkah to destroy the symbols of idolatry and propagate the faith of Islam and Monotheism. Ten thousand fully armed soldiers shared in the campaign which aimed at conquering the capital of the pagans.

Talhah ﷺ was at the head of the marching army. He was very happy to see such a huge number of Muslims marching toward Makkah. He felt that this would be the end of paganism and idolatry in the Arabian Peninsula and the start of a new stage of struggle for the sake of Islam. He thought for a while that the Prophet ﷺ would not spare any pagan and would not listen to any excuses.

Before arriving in Makkah, the Prophet ﷺ sent a messenger to Makkah to inform the inhabitants that he would like to enter the city peacefully. Hence, anyone who kept to his house or resorts to the Ka'bah would be safe.

When the Muslims controlled the city, Talhah ﷺ was astonished to hear the Prophet ﷺ granting security to all people of Makkah. He carefully listened to the merciful words of the Prophet ﷺ telling Makkans that they were free and that he would not punish them for the cruelties they had inflicted on the Muslims. Impressed with these tender words, Talhah ﷺ hugged the Prophet ﷺ and began weeping. He was sure that Muhammad ﷺ was not the type of man who fought for worldly objectives, rather he fought to bring peace to humanity.

A Bedouin came to the Prophet ﷺ asking about the words of a Verse in the Noble Qur'ân.

"What do the words 'Some of them fulfilled their obligations' mean?"

The Prophet ﷺ replied:

"Talhah is one of them."

As the Muslims finished their job in Makkah, they received news that Hawazen tribe was preparing to fight them. The Prophet ﷺ marched with a huge army to the place of Hawazen. Although the number of the Muslims was three times the number of the Hawazen tribe, they fled the battlefield. Only few devouted Companions of the Prophet ﷺ stood firm in the battlefield. Talhah ﷺ was there to loudly shout for the Muslims to come back and fight as believers. The Prophet ﷺ said to him:

"Your cry is better one hundred soldiers."

On that day, Talhah ﷺ showed rare bravery. The Prophet ﷺ looked at him and said:

"You are the abundantly generous Talhah."

★★★

The Prophet ﷺ Passes Away

Shortly after the conquest of Makkah, the Prophet ﷺ returned to Al-Madinah to prepare for pilgrimage. One hundred thousand Muslims gathered in Al-Madinah to accompany the Prophet ﷺ to Makkah. Talhah ﷺ prepared himself for this sacred journey. After completing pilgrimage rites, the Prophet ﷺ addressed his Companions at Mina. He implicitly foretold them that he might not see them after that year. Talhah ﷺ was very happy to listen to the last words by the Prophet ﷺ informing his followers that the religion of Islam had now been completed and that their mission was to spread it to the other parts of the world. However, Talhah ﷺ and many other Muslims knew that the Prophet ﷺ would not stay long among them and they all cried bitterly upon hearing the Prophet ﷺ saying:

"Maybe I would not see you after this year."

Upon returning to Al-Madinah, the Prophet ﷺ fell ill and shortly passed away. Talhah ﷺ and his brother Muslims felt that they were left without a leader and some of them could not believe that the Prophet ﷺ had left them forever.

Although Talhah ﷺ felt very sad to lose the Prophet ﷺ, he was fully aware that Allâh had now entrusted the mission of spreading the message of Islam to his followers. So, he continued his struggle for the cause of Islam and did not miss any battle fought for the sake of spreading Islam. He accompanied the Muslim army to Yarmouk to fight the Romans. He spent much of his money to provide the army with weapons and means of transportation. He was the example of a Muslim soldier that undertook the mission of fighting evil everywhere.

Talhah ﷺ spent most of his time under the rule of Abu Bakr ﷺ sharing in developing the Islamic State which was expanding day after day. He would never rest until he was sure that the faith for which he sacrificed most of his wealth and time would finally prevail.

Under the rule of 'Umar bin Al-Khattab ﷺ, Talhah ﷺ shared in organizing the affairs of the huge Islamic State and used up all his time serving the Muslim community. He always recalled those days when he was beside the Prophet ﷺ offering all he owned to support the well being of the Muslims.

After 'Umar ﷺ passed away, Talhah ﷺ continued to be the obedient soldier of Islam under the rule of 'Uthman bin 'Affan ﷺ. Now he was an old man but was still strong enough to share in spreading the Word of Allâh.

By the end of 'Uthman's rule, Talhah ﷺ was dedicating most of his time for the worship of Allâh. He longed much to leave this world clean and pious to meet Allâh on the Day of Judgment.

However, 'Uthman ﷺ was killed by some rebels. Talhah ﷺ was so concerned to see the Muslim community suffering restless days. He tried his best to bring peace to the Muslim society, after it had been torn apart by differences among faction who were supporting either Muawiyah or 'Ali رضي الله عنهما. He finally paid his life as a price to settle the issue. Those who wanted fire to remain set among Muslims killed him while he was trying his best to find an amicable settlement to end the fighting between the two factions.

High Morals

Talhah ﷺ was looked at by all the Prophet's Companions as the example of high morals and virtue. He proved eminent in all respects.

Abdur-Rahman bin 'Awf ﷺ, his partner, once asked him to allow him to irrigate his land from a well that Talhah ﷺ had in his land. Talhah ﷺ, for one reason or another, refused to do so. Abdur-Rahman ﷺ complained against Talhah ﷺ to the Prophet ﷺ. He said to Abdur-Rahman:

"How could you complain against a man whom I had told he would be in Paradise?"

Abdur-Rahman ﷺ immediately brought this good news to Talhah ﷺ. He, in return, said to Abdur-Rahman ﷺ:

"Is it worth quarreling over this unimportant property? For this news, you may have all my money, if you wish."

Talhah ﷺ was well known for his generosity. He put all his money in the service of Islam and the Muslims. One day, his wife saw that he was very upset. She asked:

"Why are you so sad?"

He said to her:

"I am upset to have all this money around me."

She immediately proposed him to spend it in charity. He,

without hesitation, called poor people and gave up all the money he had to the poor and needy.

A friend of Talhah ﷺ described him saying:

"I accompanied Talhah ﷺ for a long time. I have never seen any like him. He was always spending his money in charity."

The Martyr

At the end of 'Uthman's rule, Talhah ﷺ saw a great dilemma among the Muslims. 'Uthman bin Affân ﷺ was killed by same rebels who wanted to create conflicts in the Islamic community. Talhah ﷺ and some other Companions urged 'Ali ﷺ to take the position of the Caliph and to take revenge of 'Uthman's murder.

'Ali ﷺ on the other hand, tried to convince them that he had no idea of who was respansible for the crime and that they should wait unlil the revolt was stopped. The opposition hold their position and gathered armies to fight 'Ali ﷺ. However, Talhah ﷺ could not accept fighting among the Muslims, especially when he was convinced by 'Ali ﷺ that he was wrong. He withdrew from the battlefield and tried to settle the dispute.

The opposition did not accept such a withdrawal. Some rebels wanted the fire to remain heated. Therefore, one of the rebels shot Talhah ﷺ and killed him.

'Ali looked at the covered body and began weping. He said:

"It is terrible thing to me to see you murdered. To Allâh I complain against those who murdered him. I hoped that I would have been dead twenty years before I saw this day."

This was the end of the man who spent all his life supporting truth. It was a tragic end that nobody could expect. However, it was his destiny to be always the martyr of truth.

الزبير بن العوام رضي الله عنه

– حواري الرسول صلى الله عليه وسلم –

Az-Zubair bin Al-Awwam رضي الله عنه

The Disciple

The Orphan

Background

The Quraish tribe was comprised of several clans. The most prominent clan among them was the family of Bani Hashim. This clan had more than one religious and worldly function during the pre-Islamic period. It was notable and noble both in family lineage and position amongst the clans and tribes that inhabited Makkah. The Prophet ﷺ belonged to this clan.

Safiyah bint Abdul Muttalib, who belonged to this high-class family, finally married the notable man whom she loved and admired. She dreamt for a long time to have a son that would add to her happiness. Days were passing very slowly while she was waiting for the baby to come to this life. The bride felt she was coming closer to the day when she would be a mother.

Within the society of the Quraish, as well as other societies in the Arabian Peninsula, the household that had more male offspring was given more esteem. They felt that such boys, later on as youth, would be the ones who would protect the tribe and give the family dignity and honour.

The Dream came True

Nine months later and for the good fortune of Safiyah, she gave birth to her son. She named him Az-Zubair. From the first minute, she gave him all the care and affection that would make him a man of notable rank among his peers. The baby grew day by day and the eyes of his mother followed his steps wherever he went. Like any other mother, she considered him a piece of herself and looked at him with hope and dreams as the young man who would give her a lofty position among the women of her society.

The Orphan and his Mother

As tribes during those ancient days used to invade and be invaded by other tribes and as wars were normally waged for trivial reasons, it was ordinary for a man like Al-Awwam (Az-Zubair's father) to spend the first half of the day with his family and to become a dead body under the earth in the second half of the day. All of a sudden, Az-Zubair was left an orphan under the custody of his mother. His father had been killed in a battle among the tribes of Arabia that left nothing for many households other than mourning wives and miserable orphans.

After losing her husband, Az-Zubair's mother felt how much life was hard on her. Hence she was very keen to have recompense in her son. She ordered the boy to be trained how to use his sword and spear and how to become a man of dignity. She was very hard on him. She even beat him now and then. When she was asked why she beat him, she replied that she was doing so to make him a real man. Safiyah observed her son grow day by day. She felt very happy to learn that her son had quarreled with an adult man and had broken that man's arm. She was very proud to have a strong son.

★★★

In the Shrine of Islam

Monotheism and idolatry Face to Face

Az-Zubair grew into a strong and handsome young man. He enjoyed all the dignity and reputation that his horsemanship gave him amongst his tribesmen. He enjoyed his time with his peers. His main concern was to spend as much as he could of his time hunting and training with his sword and spear.

In addition to idolatry and setting up partners with Allâh, all the people of Makkah indulged in vices that made their life corrupt and empty of any sign of guidance from heaven. Injustices overwhelmed their acts and made the relations between the powerful and the weak tend to be tense most of the time.

In these bad conditions that prevailed in Makkah and the world in general, Muhammad bin Abdullah was sent by Allâh to preach the message of Islam. All the chiefs of the Quraish were against the message of Islam. In spite of all their cruelty, the Prophet ﷺ invited them to accept Islam to reform their society and to save them from the punishment of Allâh on the Day of Judgment. He was very merciful toward them. Although they insulted him and made his mission very difficult, he exercised patience with them. He and his few followers stood fast in the face of torture and oppression that the Quraish inflicted on them. Neither the Prophet ﷺ nor any of his followers were violent against their oppressors.

Az-Zubair and the New Message

Az-Zubair (Muhammad's cousin) saw all the agonies that the Muslims were undergoing. Although he was too young, he was sensible enough to understand what the principles of Islam meant. He, among others, listened carefully to the Prophet ﷺ and decided to adopt the new religion as a way of life.

Even before the advent of Islam, Az-Zubair was well aware of the bad condition of the people in Makkah. He felt inside himself that some sort of guidance should come to change the corrupt society of the Arabs.

On a dark night, Az-Zubair isolated himself and began thinking of those a few people who followed the new religion. He saw how much they suffered for no reason but because they held fast to their faith. The guidance that came from up high had touched his heart. He knew how much Muhammad ﷺ was honest. His mother had told him before that her nephew was famous for his truthfulness. However, after Muhammad ﷺ proclaimed Islam, she extremely opposed him. Conflicting thoughts tore his mind. He could not figure a way out of this inner conflict.

Az-Zubair kept the whole night awake. The dawn was about to break and the gentle breeze of early morning gave him new hopes. He thought that it was better to know more about the new religion from the closest man to the Prophet ﷺ. He left his home and went to Abu Bakr's house. Abu Bakr ؓ had already accepted Islam without any hesitation from the first moment the Prophet ﷺ called him to be a Muslim. Abu Bakr ؓ told Az-

Zubair that Muhammad was a true Messenger from Allâh. He explained to him the principles of Islam and urged him to follow the teachings of the Prophet ﷺ. Az-Zubair became convinced that Islam was the solution to all the problems that his society was undergoing. He immediately expressed his interest to meet the Prophet ﷺ and embrace Islam.

Az-Zubair Defends Islam

Abu Bakr ﷺ immediately took the young man to the Prophet's house. There, Az-Zubair declared that he accepted Islam. He was fifteen years old at that time. He was the fifth person to accept Islam. He pledged to defend his faith to the last moment of his life.

Day after day, the Quraish added to their oppression of the Muslims. Az-Zubair kept his acceptance of Islam secret. However, he could not stand aggression against the followers of the new religion.

While the chiefs of the Quraish were sitting near the Ka'bah mocking the Prophet ﷺ and his followers, a young man approached them crying. He began shouting that Az-Zubair had beaten up his father and had broken his arm. The young man added:

"He was about to kill my father."

He urged the chiefs of the Quraish to stop the orphan.

The chiefs of the Quraish asked the young man about the reason that made Az-Zubair beat his father. He explained:

"It was because of the difference of religion. My father had said something bad about Muhammad and Islam. Az-Zubair was angry to hear such insults because he had already accepted Islam. He beat my father and was about to kill him."

Oppression

Az-Zubair's uncle and mother tried their best to make him apologize for what they considered as misconduct. However, Az-Zubair did not even pay any attention to their threats. They urged him to abandon the new faith but he never hesitated to declare his steadfast clinging to his religion. He also called them to embrace Islam as he had done.

His mother was very hard on him to make him recant. His uncle used to wrap him with a mat and put him in smoke to suffocate him so as to make him go back to idolatry.

In spite of all hardships, Az-Zubair ﷺ kept steadfast to his belief. The more they added to his punishment, the more he held fast to his faith. He saw no difference between himself and any other Muslim subjected to pressure and agonies that would allow him to abandon his religion. Rather, he considered himself fortunate to be treated by pagans in this harsh way. He knew that such hardships would bring him closer to Allâh and make his reward on the Day of Judgment greater.

★★★

Migration to Abyssinia

No Choice but to Migrate

The Prophet ﷺ and the few early Muslims met unbearable hardships in Makkah. They were oppressed by the Quraish to the extent that they had no chance even to worship Allâh or live in peace. Muslims were mostly weak people and slaves. They had nobody to support them against the wave of oppression they were facing in Makkah.

The Muslims complained to the Prophet ﷺ. They felt that there was no choice but to leave the city or to face death. The Prophet ﷺ felt very sad for their condition but he had no power to protect them or himself against the oppression of the Quraish. Therefore, the Prophet ﷺ asked his Companions to leave to Abyssinia. He told them that land was ruled by a just and merciful Emperor. They would receive good treatment under his rule.

Leaving the Homeland

Az-Zubair ﷺ and many other Muslims left Makkah secretly to Abyssinia. When they arrived there they found the people very nice to them. They received good treatment and lived in peace. They could worship Allâh and practice their religion in the way ordained by Allâh.

When the Muslims felt secure and protected under the care

of the Emperor, they found out that an opponent of the Emperor had revolted against him. The Muslims were afraid that the rebel might seize power and overcome the Emperor. They prayed to Allâh to give victory to the Emperor.

The Emperor had to fight a big battle against his foe. The Muslims were very anxious to know the result of the battle which was about to take place behind the river Nile. They asked Az-Zubair ﷺ to go to the scene of the battle and bring them news. Az-Zubair ﷺ made a float and swam to where the battle was taking place. He saw that the Emperor had defeated his opponent and came back to his fellow Muslims with this good news. The migrants were very happy for the Emperor to defeat his enemy.

Plots against the Migrants

The chiefs of the Quraish felt that they had lost control over the Muslims. They were very angry to see the Muslims living in peace in Abyssinia. They did not like the Muslims to escape their oppression and torture. Therefore, they decided to send an envoy to the Emperor asking him to surrender the migrants back to them. They sent two envoys with gifts to the Emperor pleading him to dismiss the migrants out of his country and send them back to Makkah. The envoys tried to deceive the Emperor. They told him that the migrants said bad things about Jesus Christ. The Emperor was very wise and just. He wanted the migrants to give their testimony. He knew that the religion of these migrants was close to his religion.

The leader of the migrants, Ja'far bin Abi Tâlib ﷺ, and his fellow Muslims appeared before the Emperor. He advanced toward the Emperor and said:

"O Emperor! We were worshippers of hand carved idols. We treated each other unjustly. A man from amongst us told us that he had been sent by Allâh to take us out of the gloom of ignorance to the light of Islam. We accepted his call and believed in what he said. Our people treated us very badly. Therefore, we sought refuge in your land for we know you are just and treat your guests nicely."

The Emperor was convinced that the principles brought by Islam were a continuation of the message of previous Prophets to humanly. However, the two envoys told the Emperor that the Muslims had abandoned the religion of their forefathers. They did not follow Christianity or any other known religion and they even said bad things about Jesus Christ.

The Emperor ordered Ja'far ﷺ to tell him what they believed about Jesus. Ja'far ﷺ told the Emperor that they believed that Jesus was a messenger from and a servant of Allâh, that he was the son of Maryam the virgin and that his birth was a miracle.

The Emperor listened to Ja'far ﷺ very carefully. As Ja'far was reciting *Âyât* (Verses) of the Qur'ân from *Sûrah Maryam*, the eyes of the Emperor were filled with tears. He told the men around him that the things Ja'far said about Jesus were the same as what Jesus said about himself.

He ordered the gifts brought by the delegation of the Quraish to be given back to them and dismissed them. He told them that he would never surrender the Muslims to them. He turned his face toward the Muslims and told them that they were free to live in his land and to worship Allâh as they liked.

The chiefs of the Quraish were disappointed to know that

the Emperor of Abyssinia took the side of the Muslims. However, they changed their plots. They spread rumours here and there that they had concluded an agreement with the Prophet ﷺ and that they would not challenge the Muslims. Some migrants believed the rumours and returned to Makkah. However, they found out that this news was false. Some of them were captured by the Quraish but others escaped again and returned to Abyssinia.

Emigration to Al-Madinah

The Prophet ﷺ and the Muslims who stayed in Makkah received all kinds of oppression by the Quraish. However, the Prophet ﷺ kept proclaiming the message of Islam to members of tribes who came to Makkah as pilgrims. In the beginning, all attempts to have atribe to support the Muslims and protect them against oppression failed. Most of the tribes living in the suburbs of Makkah were afraid to follow the teachings of the Prophet ﷺ or provide any help to the Muslims lest the Quraish wage war agthem.

Al-Madinah people accept Islam

In his efforts of calling people to Islam, the Prophet ﷺ met some pilgrims from a town four hundred kilometers away from Makkah called Yathrib. These people had already heard of the close appearance of a new Prophet ﷺ in Arabia. The Jews who were living in the suburbs of Yathrib used to threaten them that a new Prophet ﷺ would appear, that they would follow and support him and that they would conquer the Arabs. The pilgrims from Yathrib kept this threat in mind. When they heard of the Prophet ﷺ, they met him and listened to his preaching. They were finally convinced that the man was a real Messenger from Allâh and that it was better for them to accept Islam.

The few men accepted Islam and promised the Prophet ﷺ to announce it in Yathrib. They also agreed with the Prophet ﷺ to come next year to make a pledge of protection of Islam and Muslims. Some seventy men and women came to Makkah the following year and pledged to support the Prophet ﷺ and his Companions.

Secret migration

With the increase of hardships on the Muslims, the Prophet ﷺ and his Companions had no other option but to leave Makkah to Yathrib. The Prophet ﷺ instructed his Companions to emigrate to Yathrib secretly. When he was sure that no weak Muslims remained in Makkah, the Prophet ﷺ and his closest Companion, Abu Bakr ؓ, also left Makkah secretly.

Az-Zubair joins his fellow Muslims

Az-Zubair ؓ and his companions in Abyssinia received news that the Muslims had finally found refuge in Al-Madinah. Therefore, they left to Al-Madinah to join in building the new Islamic State. Upon arriving in Al-Madinah, Az-Zubair ؓ discovered that his mother had already accepted Islam and emigrated with the other Muslims. He was so happy to meet the Prophet ﷺ and his mother under the banner of Islam.

Az-Zubair ؓ settled with his wife in Al-Madinah. They both shared with other Muslims, both emigrants and supporters, in establishing foundations for the strong Islamic State.

Wars against the new Islamic State

No sooner did the Muslims settle in Al-Madinah than pagans started attempts to tumble the new state. At the same time, they were permitted by Allâh to fight the pagans and spred the light of Islam around Al-Madinah. The Muslims began patrolling outside Al-Madinah for security perposes. They received the news that a caravan belonging to the Quraish was bound to Makkah back from Damasucs nearby Al-Madinah. They went it to check it. The leader of the caravan, Abu Sufyan, knew of the Muslims' plans and changed his direction to escape their catch. As a caution, he sent a messenger to Makkah to warn the Quraish and get their help to save the caravan. The chiefs of Quraish got very angry to hear this news. They prepared an army of one thousand fully armed men. They wanted to destroy the new state and put an end to the threats of the Muslims. Although they were assured by Abu Sufyan that the caravan was safe and intact and that there was no need to engage in combat and blood shed, they were driven by their arrogance and insisted on proceeding in their evil effort.

The Muslims, on the other side, barely could gather three hundred and thirteen poorly armed men. However, their trust in Allâh was very strong. They knew that they were right and the pagans were wrong.

Both armies met at a place near to Al-Madinah called Badr. The Muslims reached the place before the pagans. They ruined all sources of water that the Quraish army might use and kept some basins under their protection for their own use.

Soon fighting started very fiercely. Although the Muslims were outnumbered by the pagans, they defeated them in no time. Seventy men from the Quraish were killed and a similar number caught as prisoners of war.

Az-Zubair ﷺ shared in the first battle waged against Islam. He did his best to protect his faith and his state. He was young, strong and eager to put an end to the tyranny of the pagans.

A year later, the Quraish wanted to take revenge for the big blow they received at Badr. They gathered three thousand fighters and headed toward Al-Madinah with false hopes of putting an end to Islam and the Muslims.

Both the Muslim and pagan armies met at a place near to Al-Madinah called Uhud Mount. Hypocrites, led by Abdullah bin Ubay, played a major role in weakening the Muslim army. A third of the Muslim army had withdrawn from the battle scene before the battle started. However, the Muslims fought with zeal and steadfast faith. At the beginning of the battle they were defeating the pagan army. The archers, whom the Prophet ﷺ positioned over a small hill near the battle scene to protect the backs of the Muslim army, thought that it was a final defeat. As a result, they disobeyed the orders of their leader, went down the hill and began collecting war booty. The horsemen of the Quraish took the chance and attacked the Muslim army from behind. Hence, they turned the defeat to a virtual victory.

The Brave Fighter

Az-Zubair ﷺ and some other Companions of the Prophet ﷺ kept steadfast and protected the Prophet ﷺ against attempts to kill him. He stood in the middle of the battlefield shooting arrows at the pagan fighters until the battle was over. His uncle Hamza ﷺ was killed in the battle and his body was mutilated. His mother came to see the body of her brother, but the Prophet ﷺ told him to stop her. She was a true Muslim and told her son that she knew that her brother's body was deformed by the pagans and that she would keep patient for she knew that her brother's soul would go to Paradise.

As the Quraish could not achieve their intentions, they started preparing for another final battle. They held a pact against Islam and the Muslims and gathered ten thousand soldiers from all over

Arabia. They again headed toward Al-Madinah.

Courage in times of Hardships

Muslims, on the other hand, felt the danger and discussed the best way to defend their town and people. Finally, a Muslim from Persia named Salman Al-Farsi ﷺ devised a plan that would provide protection for the town. He advised the Muslims to dig a trench around the town so as to prevent the pagans from entering the town. The Prophet ﷺ and his Companions welcomed the idea and began working on the trench.

Az-Zubair ﷺ joined hands with his fellow Muslims in digging the trench. He was working all the day long to complete the job before the pagan army arrived in Al-Madinah. Finally, he and his brothers completed the work and prepared themselves to fight the advancing army. The Jews, being jealous to see Islam spread so swiftly and gain power every day, promised the pagans to help them against the Muslims. Hence, the Muslims were stuck in the middle between the two forces.

The pagans arrived at the outskirts of Al-Madinah. To their utmost surprise, they were stopped by the trench and the Muslim archers were ready to shoot down any trespasser. The Prophet ﷺ sent an envoy to the Jews asking them help as they had already held a treaty with Muslims to help each other at the times of crisis. However, the Jews treated the envoy very rudely and told him that they had broken their covenants.

The pagan army kept surrounding Al-Madinah for about one month. The Muslim children, women and elderly were kept inside a fenced placed lest the Jews or pagans cause harm to them. Safiya رضي الله عنها, Az-Zubair's mother, was at that place. She saw a Jew roaming around the place. She was afraid that he might come in and attack any of them. She took a long stick, surprised the Jew and killed him.

The pagan army lost all hope of penetrating the trench. Their leader, Abu Sufyan, ordered them to leave. Az-Zubair ﷺ and his fellow Muslims were very happy to see the high wind blow through the pagan army's tents. He knew it was a help from Allâh to the Muslims.

Only Az-Zubair ﷺ can do it

The Prophet ﷺ wanted to get news about the enemy. He inquired who would be the man to go to their tents in the night and come back with news. Az-Zubair ﷺ expressed his wish to be the man. The Prophet ﷺ repeated his request and Az-Zubair ﷺ was the man who volunteered himself for the mission. The third time the Prophet ﷺ permitted him to perform the task and said:

"Every Prophet has a disciple. My disciple is Az-Zubair."

Now the Muslims had to settle their case with the deceiving Jews (Bani Quraithah). They besieged their homes and forced them to surrender. Az-Zubair and 'Ali bin Abi Tâlib رضي الله عنهما climbed the walls of their fortress and opened the gates for the Muslims to capture it. The Bani Quraithah men were sentenced to death and their women and children were taken as slaves. That was the just reward for their deception and breaking of promises.

Az-Zubair's wife added to Az-Zubair's happiness when she gave birth to a child whom they named Abdullah. Abdullah was to become one of the great Companions of the Prophet ﷺ and sacrifice his life for the cause of Islam. He was the first boy born to the Muslims in Al-Madinah.

The Brave Soldier

Day after day, Az-Zubair ﷺ and his brothers in Islam established a fairly strong state in Al-Madinah with the help of Allâh and under the leadership of the Prophet ﷺ. They started inviting other tribes to Islam and deterring any tribe that tried to assault them.

Visit to the Holy Land

Az-Zubair ﷺ and his fellow Muslims were informed by the Prophet ﷺ that they should perform pilgrimage. The Prophet ﷺ and many of his Companions marched to Makkah barely armed. The Quraish received news of the Muslims' march. They asked some of their horsemen to prevent the Muslims from entering Makkah.

The Muslims camped at a place called Hudaybiya. The chiefs of the Quraish sent their envoys to the Prophet ﷺ to inquire about the reason they came to Makkah. They knew that the Muslims wanted to perform pilgrimage peacefully. The pagans denied the Muslims this chance. They negotiated an agreement with the Prophet ﷺ to stop war for ten years and to permit the Muslims to perform pilgrimage the coming year.

However, the Quraish failed to respect their word. They attacked some of the Muslims's allies and killed as many as forty of them. The Prophet ﷺ knew of the Quraish's breach of the agreement and decided to conquer Makkah. It was a big stride forward. The Muslims prepared themselves to conquer the city and put an end to idolatry.

The Conqueror

Az-Zubair led the left wing of the army and marched to Makkah under the leadership of the Prophet ﷺ. Ten thousand Muslims were ready to fight their last battle against the idolaters in Arabia. Before conquering the city, the Prophet ﷺ announced that the Muslims did not wish to shed any blood. Hence, he declared that if no resistance was made, all Makkans would be safe and secure. Upon entering Makkah, Az-Zubair ﷺ advanced toward the Prophet ﷺ and cleaned dust from the Prophet's blessed face.

Mercy of Islam

Az-Zubair ﷺ longed much to revenge himself on those who oppressed him and his brothers in Islam. However, he had no choice but to obey the orders of the Prophet ﷺ. He was witness to the merciful position of the Prophet ﷺ toward the pagans. As Muslims cleaned the vicinity of the Ka'bah from idols, the Prophet ﷺ stood on a high place and inquired how the Quraish expected he would treat them. They all replied that they knew he would be merciful to them. He assured them and told them that they were free and no harm would befall them.

Expansion over Arabia

As the Muslims finished with their job in Makkah, they received news that Hawazen tribe in Tâ'if were preparing to fight against them. The Prophet ﷺ commanded his Companions to march to Tâ'if and conquer Hawazen. The Muslims felt that they had become very strong. Some of them said:

"No one on earth can defeat us from now on."

As they met the army of Hawazen, many of them fled from the battle scene. Only the Prophet ﷺ, Az-Zubair ؓ and a few other Companions of the Prophet ﷺ kept their positions and bravely fought a big battle. The leader of Hawazen saw a tall man penetrating their rows. He inquired who was that man. They told him that the man was Az-Zubair ؓ. He praised him and asked his men to show bravery. Finally, the Muslims, thanks to the steadfast position taken by the Prophet ﷺ and his sincere Companions, returned to the battlefield and defeated their enemy.

Az-Zubair ؓ continued his struggle for the cause of Islam. The Prophet ﷺ received news that the Romans in Syria were angry to know that Muslims conquered all of Arabia. They were intent to invade the Islamic State. The Prophet ﷺ ordered his Companions to march to Jordan before the Romans entered Arabia. Three thousand soldiers marched to Muta, a place on the northern borders of Arabia. Az-Zubair ؓ fought a big battle and with his fellow Muslims showed the Romans how strong the Muslims had become.

He was also in the front lines when the Prophet ﷺ commanded his Companions to march to the north borders of Arabia to deter the Romans again. He shared in Tabuk excursion in the hot season of summer and performed his duties to the best of his ability.

When the Prophet ﷺ passed away, Az-Zubair ؓ felt very sad to lose his leader and teacher. However, he continued his efforts to spread the message of Islam and implement the teachings of the leader.

Steadfast to the End

Abu Bakr was elected as Caliph (ruler) immediately after the Prophet had passed away. Arabs around Makkah and remote areas revolted against the Muslims and apostated. Az-Zubair was one of the leaders who subdued the apostates and brought order again to the Islamic State. He fought all those who attempted to stop the light of Allâh.

Az-Zubair considered himself a soldier of Islam. He always joined the Muslim army to fight against disbelievers. He shared in the Yarmuk battle against the Romans. The Muslim army defeated the Romans and liberated Syria.

One man Equal to one thousand Men

Az-Zubair was well known for his courage and skill in wars. He used his sword for the support of Islam in case there had been any aggression against Islam or the Muslims. After the death of Abu Bakr, 'Umar bin Al-Khattab was selected as Caliph. He gave his orders to 'Amr bin Al-'Aas to conquer Egypt. The Romans in Egypt were oppressing the people. He was told by the Caliph that his mission was to liberate it from their unjust rule. After conquering most part of Egypt, 'Amr bin Al-'Aas asked the Caliph to send him supplies and support. 'Umar sent four men to him, one of whom was Az-Zubair. He told him that these four men were equal to four thousand soldiers.

'Umar bin Al-Khattab chose Az-Zubair as one of the six persons who would possibly be the next Caliph after him.

This selection shows the rank that Az-Zubair ﷺ had among the Companions of the Prophet ﷺ. All the senior Companions of the Prophet ﷺ consulted among themselves and finally selected 'Uthman bin 'Affan ﷺ to be the Caliph. Az-Zubair ﷺ continued his endeavours under the rule of 'Uthman ﷺ in spreading the light of Islam. He joined the Muslim army wherever it was dispatched to liberate human beings from the worship of false deities and turn them to the worship of the One Allâh.

The True Disciple

Az-Zubair bin Al-Awwam رضي الله عنه was distinct among the Companions of the Prophet ﷺ for his good character and true loyalty to the Prophet ﷺ and Islam. He was one of the early Muslims in Makkah. He was also one of the Companions whom the Prophet ﷺ foretold would be in Paradise on the Day of Judgment. Foremost, he was the disciple of the Prophet ﷺ.

Defending his Leader and Teacher

Az-Zubair رضي الله عنه was very loyal to the Prophet ﷺ. Once he heard rumors that the pagans had killed the Prophet ﷺ. He took his sword and wanted to fight them. However, when he saw the Prophet ﷺ alive, he hugged him and was extremely happy. The Prophet ﷺ, in return, took off his cloak and gave it to Az-Zubair رضي الله عنه. The angel Gabriel, told the Prophet ﷺ that Allâh was pleased to see Az-Zubair رضي الله عنه act with zeal in defending the Prophet ﷺ.

'Umar bin Al-Khattab رضي الله عنه described Az-Zubair رضي الله عنه as one of the pillars of Islam. He was sincerely devoted to the cause of Islam. A friend of Az-Zubair told that once he saw the body of Az-Zubair رضي الله عنه with many scars; all due to cuts made by swords as a result of fighting in the way of Allâh.

Az-Zubair رضي الله عنه always kept close to the Prophet ﷺ . Even when the Prophet ﷺ was sleeping, he kept beside him to protect him against enemies. The Prophet ﷺ once slept and Az-Zubair رضي الله عنه sat beside him to keep flies away from his blessed face. The Prophet ﷺ woke up and saw Az-Zubair ﷺ using a fan to expel flies from his face. He told Az-Zubair ﷺ that he would be with Az-Zubair ﷺ on the Day of Judgment to protect him against the sparks of hellfire.

Fear from Hellfire

It is known that many of the Prophet's sayings were reported to us by his Companions. They have memorized nearly every word he preached to them in various fields of life and *Shari'ah* (Islamic law). Az-Zubair always kept close to the Prophet ﷺ and memorized many of *Ahadith* (Prophet's sayings). However, he only reported a very few number of the Prophet's sayings. As he was very close to the Prophet ﷺ, his son Abdullah exclaimed why should his father not report the Prophet's sayings. Az-Zubair ﷺ told his son that he was afraid he might tell something wrong. He always recalled the Prophet ﷺ warning:

> "Anyone who tells lies when he reports my sayings, his position will be in hellfire."

Az-Zubair ﷺ never feared to become indebted for he knew that Allâh would be on his side. He told his son that whenever he felt the burden of debts, he should pray to the Lord to pay his debt.

The Martyr

Immediately after 'Uthman bin 'Affan ﷺ was killed by the rebels, Az-Zubair and Talhah رضي الله عنهما felt that the Islamic state would be disrupted if no Caliph is selected to control the conditions of the State. They, with many other senior Companions of the Prophet ﷺ came to 'Ali bin Abi Tâlib ﷺ

and insisted on him to take over. After several attempts, 'Ali ﷺ accepted their proposal. Az-Zubair ﷺ came back to Makkah. He met 'Âishah, رضي الله عنها the Prophet's wife. She told him that the murderers of 'Uthman ﷺ should be killed. Az-Zubair ﷺ was convinced that a murderer should, according to Islamic Law, be killed. He agreed with her and both wanted 'Ali ﷺ to accept their proposal.

However, 'Ali ﷺ did not like to establish feuding among the Muslims in such a critical situation. He did not accept their proposal. Az-Zubair ﷺ and many others insisted on having 'Uthman's killers killed. A war broke out behind this dispute between 'Ali and Muawiyah رضي الله عنهما.

Accepting Truth when it is Clear

A war was about to break between 'Ali and Az-Zubair رضي الله عنهما because 'Ali ﷺ did not agree to his point of view that the rebels should be brought to justice. 'Ali ﷺ wanted Az-Zubair ﷺ and others to wait until the turmoil was over in order that he could distinguish the murderers.

A war was about to break and both men met face to face again. 'Ali ﷺ asked Az-Zubair ﷺ to meet together to discuss the situation and find out a solution instead of fighting. 'Ali ﷺ met Az-Zubair ﷺ and reminded him of past days when the Prophet ﷺ was alive. He said:

> "Don't you remember when the Prophet ﷺ was walking with you and I met you? Didn't he tell you that you will unjustly fight against me?"

Az-Zubair ﷺ immediately left the battle scene and went back to Makkah. He did not like to fight against 'Ali ﷺ because he remembered those words told to him by the Prophet ﷺ. However, the traitors did not like such an act. They followed him on the way to Makkah and killed him while he was praying.

The killers thought that they had done something good. They came to 'Ali ﷺ with the something good. They came to 'Ali ﷺ with the news of Az-Zubair's death. 'Ali ﷺ felt very sad for the death of Az-Zubair ﷺ and prayed to Allâh to punish those who killed him. Az-Zubair ﷺ was buried on the way from Iraq to Makkah. He said:

> "May Allâh gather us together on Doomsday in Paradise."

This was the end of the noble man who spent all his life fighting for the cause of Allâh. May Allâh bestow his mercy on Az-Zubair ﷺ for his services to Islam and the Muslims.

عمــرو بن العــاص رضي الله عنه
- فـاتــح المصــر -

'Amr bin Al-'Aas رضي الله عنه

The Conqueror of Egypt

The Most Cunning Opponet

Background

Like other first class men, 'Amr bin Al-'Aas was brought up in a high ranking house in Makkah. Since childhood, he showed signs of cleverness that his society highly appreciated. He was trained with his fellow youngsters on how to use his sword to defend his tribe and how to use his mind to foil the plots of enemies. He dedicated all his physical and mental powers for this end. He was known since he was a boy to be of high mental capabilities reflected in shrewd thinking and sound planning. While still young, 'Amr established close relations with several kings and governors of lands in and out of the Arabian Peninsula. Among those kings was the Emperor of Abyssinia and other high ranking persons whom he approached in due course to achieve his goals.

Opposition to Islam

When the Prophet Muhammad ﷺ was ordered to proclaim the new religion of Islam, most leaders of the Quraish opposed the new religion. They did their best and used most of their resources to kill the newborn faith while still fresh. They used to worshipp idols and do bad acts which they did not want to abandon. In addition, they felt that the new religion would strip them of their privileges over their slaves and other weak people. This opposition largely depended on oppression and harassment of the followers of Islam who were mostly slaves and weak persons.

'Amr bin Al-'Aas, like other high class tribesmen, shared in the attempts to put an end to the call of Islam. He spared no means to make the life of the Muslims in Makkah as hard as possible. His plans to bring the Muslims to the verge of despair discouraged many people, who believed in the new religion, from making their decision known to others.

The Miserable Envoy

As the challenge was immense, the early weak Muslims had no choice but to seek refuge and protection against the torture they received at the hands of the chiefs of the Quraish. Therefore, they asked the Prophet ﷺ to find them a place where they could find protection and refuge from increasing oppression. The Prophet ﷺ ordered his Companions to migrate to Abyssinia in Africa. He told them that the King of Abyssinia would treat them with justice.

Many of the early Muslims migrated to that land in the hope to live in peace and worship the One Allâh as ordained by the religion of Islam.

The leaders of the Quraish knew of the move. They did their best to prevent the Muslims from leaving Makkah. They detained some of their slaves who had already believed in Islam and added to their agonies. They wanted to keep the Muslims under their control. Many Muslims were confined to their homes and subjected to great oppression.

The Muslims who migrated to Abyssinia received nice treatment by the King of Abyssinia and finally found shelter from the bad treatment of their oppressors. The leaders of the Quraish found that many Muslims had escaped from their control. They finally admitted that they had lost this battle. Therefore, they sought to make the King of Abyssinia expel the migrants back to Makkah. They consulted the best way to influence the King of Abyssinia to regain control over the Muslims who sought refuge in his country. They decided to send a delegation to the King, especially since they had good commercial relations with him and his people.

When the Quraish reached a decision to bring the Muslims back to Makkah, they looked for suitable man to make the attempt successful. They finally selected 'Amr bin Al-'Aas for this mission. They knew well his shrewdness and eloquence not to mention his good relationship with the King.

'Amr accepted the mission with zeal and decided to cause as much harm as he could to the Muslims' cause. He headed to Abyssinia with the intention to bring back the migrants in chains. As soon as he reached there, he met the men of the court and priests. He asked them to speak bad about the migrants before the King. He gave them several presents, which they liked very much and thanked him for his nice gesture. After a while, he asked to meet the King himself. The King welcomed him and accepted his gifts with joy. He inquired about the reasons that brought 'Amr to his country. 'Amr explained to him that some fugitives had sought refuge in the King's land. He claimed that they had abandoned their peoples' religion and brought shame to their honour. 'Amr pleaded the King to arrest them and get them expelled back to Makkah.

The King was known for his justice and wisdom. He asked

'Amr to allow him time to think the case over. He also set a day to hear from both the Quraish's delegation and the migrants.

The migrants led by Ja'far bin Abi Tâlib ﷺ knew of the plot. However, they decided to defend their case and to tell the King the truth about their beliefs. They discussed the best way to challenge the plots of the delegation sent by the Quraish.

On the stipulated day and time, both sides appeared before the King. The Quraish's delegation led by 'Amr bin Al-'Aas were given the chance to present their accusations against the migrants. 'Amr delivered his claims against the Muslims saying:

"O King, some insolent persons have sought refuge in your country. They have deviated from the religion of their forefathers, have not accepted your religion and have brought about an innovated religion unknown to you and to us. Their people have sent you their fathers and uncles to ask you to force them to go back to their people, for they best know how to deal with them."

The King, Najâshi, did not take 'Amr's words for granted and objected to expel the refugees unless he heard their testimony. He turned to the side of the migrants and inquired about the religion that made them abandon other known religions. Ja'far bin Abi Tâlib ﷺ stepped forward to explain the plea of the migrants. He said:

"O King, we were idol worshippers. We were doing vices, cutting relations with our blood relatives and insulting our neighbours. The powerful amongst us badly treated the weak. Allâh has sent us a Messenger from among ourselves whom we know very well. He is of good ancestry, honest and trustworthy. He urged us to worship Allâh Alone and abandon worshipping idols made of stone. He told us to say truth, to be trustworthy, to be good to our relatives and neighbours, to abstain from doing vices and murdering each other and to stop usurping orphans' properties. We believed in him and followed his teachings. We began worshipping the One Allâh and abstained from doing evil things. However, our people did not leave us alone. They oppressed us and wanted us to go back to old evils. They treated us very badly and left us no way to practice our religion and hence forced us to migrate to your land, where we hope we would be treated with justice."

The King listened carefully to these nice words and finally inquired if Ja'far ﷺ could tell him of any revelations sent down by Allâh to their Prophet ﷺ. Ja'far ﷺ immediately started reciting some Verses of the Noble Qur'ân.

Upon hearing a few Verses, the King's tears ran down his beard and even the monks shared in this highly spiritual moment. He addressed the Quraish's delegation saying:

"You know that these words and those revealed unto Jesus come from one source. Go back to your people for I will never surrender these people to you."

Insisting on harming the Muslims

'Amr felt very angry to lose this round against the Muslims. He felt that his plot was failed. However, he started considering another way to seed doubt in the heart of the King about the beliefs of the migrants.

On the next day, he requested to meet the King again. He told him that the migrants said something bad about Jesus Christ. The King again ordered for the migrants to be brought before him to hear from them.

The migrants thought that the King had changed his mind and that he would surrender them to the delegation of the Quraish.

The migrants gathered and appeared before the King. Najâshi asked Ja'far ﷺ about the things they said about Jesus. He immediately replied that the Noble Qur'ân told them that Jesus was Allâh's servant, His word and spirit given to Maryam. The King then asked if Ja'far could prove his statement. Ja'far immediately began reciting some of the Verses of the Qur'ân from *Sûrah Maryam* describing Jesus Christ and how he was born.

As Ja'far ﷺ completed reciting the Verses of the Qur'ân, the King said:

"By Allâh, what we have about Jesus is exactly the same these people have. These are the things Jesus himself said about himself."

He addressed the Muslims saying:

"You will be safe in my land as long as I am alive. Whoever causes harm to you, he would surely be a loser. Had I have been given a mount of gold to cause harm to you, I would have rejected it."

He again turned toward the Quraish's delegation and told

them that he would not accept their gifts for he would not accept any bribe against the Muslims.

At this moment, 'Amr realized for the first time that his shrewdness was of no avail. It was Allâh who protected the migrants against his plots. He surely felt inside himself that something unusual made the migrants win this battle against him and the Quraish.

'Amr returned to Makkah disappointed. He and other chiefs of the Quraish thought of another trick to make the migrants come back to Makkah by themselves. The Quraish spread rumors that they had made an agreement with Muhammad ﷺ and that no more oppression would be inflicted on the Muslims.

Some of the migrants believed the rumors and came back to Makkah. These Muslims were caught by the Quraish and subjected to more torture. Other Muslims fled again to Abyssinia and stayed there until the Prophet ﷺ and his Companions migrated to Al-Madinah.

Still living in Darkness

'Amr continued his fighting against the Muslims and used all means to undermine the new Faith. He and other chiefs of the Quraish tried to prevent the Muslims from emigrating to Al-Madinah. Even after many of the Muslims had emigrated to Al-Madinah, the bitter enemies of Islam plotted to kill the Prophet ﷺ. They agreed to have one person from every tribe in and around Makkah to share in killing the Prophet ﷺ. Forty young men stood by the Prophet's house on the night he was ordered by Allâh to migrate to Al-Madinah. However, Allâh saved the Prophet ﷺ from their plots.

Warring against Islam

'Amr continued his war against Islam and the Muslims. As soon as he knew that the Muslims who settled in Al-Madinah had threatened their trade caravan, he prepared himself to attack them in Al-Madinah. He convinced the people of Makkah that it was time to stop the threat of Islam. He and other chefs of the Quraish prepared an army of one thousand fully armed soldiers and marched to Al-Madinah in an attempt to put off the light of Islam. However, when the battle started he lost all his cunning and shrewdness. Again, he lost his battle against the Muslims at the battle of Badr.

'Amr still did not realize that the Muslims were supported by a divine power. He continued in the same way of opposition to Islam. He and other chiefs of the Quraish convinced Abu Sufyan to use the revenues of the trade caravan which had escaped from the hands of the Muslims to finance their coming battle against the Muslims.

More and more challenges to Islam

'Amr and other chiefs of the Quraish gathered an army of three thousand soldiers and marched to Al-Madinah. They thought that they would revenge themselves against the Muslims and put an end to the message of Islam. Even women participated in the march. 'Amr and other horsemen of the Quraish led the army near to Al-Madinah. In spite of their little number compared to the army of the Quraish, the Muslims defeated their enemy in the beginning of the battle. However, the archers whom the Prophet ﷺ positioned over a small hill behind the Muslim army to protect their backs came down and joined the other members of the army in collecting war booty. 'Amr and Khalid bin Al-Waleed turned from behind the Muslim army and attacked them. Although they defeated the Muslims in this battle, their aims to destroy Islam did not succeed.

As 'Amr returned to Makkah, he began preparing for another battle against the Muslims. He used his shrewdness to convince most of the Arab tribes in Arabia to join the Quraish in their final battle against the Muslims. Even the Jews, who were closer to the Muslims in belief than to pagans, shared in the efforts to gather a huge army of ten thousand soldiers. They were intent on attacking Al-Madinah and destroying the new Islamic State. 'Amr led the army to Al-Madinah, but to his astonishment, he found a wide trench separating him and his army from the town. The Muslims used this military trick to deter the attackers. The pagan army spent twenty-five days surrounding Al-Madinah, but they failed to cross over the trench. At last, they left back in humiliation.

At this moment of time 'Amr felt that Islam was not something invented by Muhammad ﷺ, otherwise, it would have not been able to live within this hostile environment. He wanted to change his mind and join the Muslims, but the feeling of arrogance kept him away from following the path of truth.

'Amr spent a long period of time thinking of what to do in the face of the advancement of Islam. His attempts had all been failed. The Muslims were now very strong. In spite of all battles he waged against them, he did not stop their march.

★★★

A Pause before Submission

In spite of the fact that 'Amr had been a hard opponent of Islam, he should have thought once that all his efforts to undermine the new religion had ended in vain. He should have mediated how could such a small group of weak and oppressed people overcome the challenge of the Quraish and other Arabs had it not been for something divine supporting them. However, 'Amr was still doubting the truthfulness of the new faith, for he was brought up among the leaders of the Quraish who found their status and power weakened by the message of Islam.

The plotter himself seeking Refuge

Upon returning defeated to Makkah after ending the siege against Al-Madinah, 'Amr was fully sure that the new religion would finally triumph over all other opponents. Hence, he decided to seek refuge before he was caught by Muhammad ﷺ and his followers. He suggested to a group of his friends to leave to Abyssinia where his friend, the King, might provide protection to him until the battle with Muhammad ﷺ and his Companions was over.

'Amr and his friends collected some gifts and headed to Abyssinia where they were welcomed by the King. He spent a period of time there thinking of how to find a way out of the plight he had entangled himself in. He even once asked the

King to surrender the Prophet's representative to him to kill him so as to quench his thirst for revenge against the Muslims. However, the King angrily blamed him for such a request. Upon hearing these words from the King, 'Amr began thinking seriously that he was on the wrong track. He listened carefully to the King advising him to follow the Prophet Muhammad ﷺ. The King added:

> "He will overcome those who oppose him as Moses overcame the Pharaoh and his soldiers."

Deliberation

'Amr asked the Emperor whether he would join him in accepting Islam. The king affirmed that he accepted Islam as his religion before Allâh. 'Amr left the royal court astonished to hear these words from the King. He realized that Muhammad ﷺ was not a man proclaiming Islam for something personal. He saw him in Makkah and knew how much he was truthful and trustworthy. He also felt how much his followers were sincere to their faith, in spite of all the agonies that they suffered. How could a wise and a clever man like him keep himself blind to the values and morals that Muhammad ﷺ preached to the people of Makkah? How long should he stick to idols which he had been asking to give but they never responded to him?

He was well aware of the fact that if he sought Muhammad's help, he would be welcomed as a new brother of Islam. Hence, he deeply questioned himself about the reasons that kept him away from being a Muslim for this long time. He spent many days thinking about Muhammad ﷺ and Islam and finally reached a decision. There was no way but to migrate to Al-

Madinah and embrace the religion of Islam.

On the way to Islam

'Amr kept his decision to migrate to Al-Madinah and to embrace Islam secret. He prepared himself and left for Al-Madinah. On the way there, he met Khalid bin Al-Waleed and 'Uthmân bin Talhah. He inquired about the reason that brought them this way. Khalid answered that it had become very clear to him that Muhammad ﷺ was a true Messenger of Allâh and that they were leaving to Al-Madinah to embrace Islam. 'Amr confirmed Khalid's words and informed him that he was also going there to follow Islam. "Since our destination and objective is the same, and we had lost our way in the same manner, why don't we travel together?" Talking on topics of common interest they reached Al-Madinah in the ninth of Safar on 8th Hijrah.

Since some time before accepting Islam, in his mind, 'Amr bin Al-'Aas ﷺ had begun to feel a liking and inclination towards this pure religion. But the authority and influence of his father, and the arrogance and pride of the Quraish, had stood in his way from openly declaring himself a Muslim.

As soon as 'Amr and his companions reached Al-Madinah, they went to the mosque where the Prophet ﷺ was preaching to his followers. As he finished his session, 'Amr advanced to the Prophet ﷺ. He looked at the face of the Prophet ﷺ and felt a shiver go through his body. He was afraid that the Prophet ﷺ might punish him for his past plots against Islam. To his surprise, the Prophet ﷺ smiled at him and hugged him warmly. 'Amr immediately announced his acceptance of Islam. The

Prophet ﷺ said that Makkah had thrown its favourite sons towards them.

'Amr also asked the Prophet ﷺ to pray to Allâh to forgive him his past sins. The Prophet ﷺ replied that whenever one becomes a Muslim all his past sins would be forgiven. The Prophet ﷺ asked his Companions to welcome the new Muslim and teach him how to pray. He also asked them to provide all means of help to the new comer. 'Amr's heart was filled with love of the Prophet ﷺ and his Companions for their attitude toward him. He understood well that they were not struggling for worldly things, rather their aims were to bring all human beings under the merciful umbrella of Islam.

'Amr the Muslim

From the day 'Amr accepted Islam, his mission had changed from fighting against Islam to fighting for the sake of Islam. He remained by the side of the Prophet ﷺ supporting the message of Islam and spared no effort to make it victorious.

The Muslim Leader

In the eighth year after the migration to Al-Madinah, there were still some clans around Al-Madinah who caused some harm to the Muslims. Now and then, their men attacked the suburbs of Al-Madinah and robbed some camels and killed some Muslims. Other tribes also held pacts with the Romans to weaken the march of Islam toward the northern parts of the Arabian Peninsula.

'Amr ﷺ knew very well the locations of these tribes. He also knew how to stop their threats to the Muslims.

The Prophet ﷺ selected 'Amr ﷺ to lead a small army to subdue the Arab tribes who tried to cause harm to the Muslims. He could punish these tribes and stop their efforts to harm the Muslims. 'Amr ﷺ also led several Muslim brigades throughout Arabia. He successfully undermined the plans of enemies and put an end to their plots against the Muslims.

The conquest of Makkah

'Amr ﷺ was a witness to the peace treaty that the Prophet ﷺ concluded with the Quraish at Al-Hudaibiyah. At that moment he was at the side of the pagans. However, the pagans failed to respect the treaty. They attacked the Muslims and killed some forty men and women.

The Prophet ﷺ had no choice but to retaliate. It was time to put an end to idolatry in the Arabian Peninsula and to spread the light of Islam in the centre of Arabia.

On the day when the Prophet ﷺ headed to Makkah to conquer the capital of the Quraish, 'Amr ﷺ was at his side. He thought that the Prophet ﷺ would avenge himself against the chiefs of the Quraish. However he forgot how merciful the Prophet ﷺ was to him. He witnessed how much the Prophet ﷺ was merciful to those who did their best to stop his call to Islam. As soon as the Prophet ﷺ finished his job in Makkah, he ordered 'Amr ﷺ to destroy Suwa', an idol worshipped by a mighty Arab tribe named Huzail. 'Amr ﷺ did the job successfully and convinced the people there to embrace Islam.

The tribe of Hawazin near Makkah collected a huge army and prepared themselves to fight the Muslims. The Prophet ﷺ led the Muslims to deter Hawazin. The two armies met at a place called Hunain. 'Amr ﷺ fought along with the Muslims. He was astonished to see the Muslims flee from the battlefield. Only a few Muslims including the Prophet ﷺ held fast to their positions. They fled because they said that from now on they would never be conquered. The Prophet ﷺ called them to return to their positions and the Muslims finally won the battle.

'Amr ﷺ also shared with the Prophet ﷺ in the excursion to Tabuk to deter the Romans and their allies who were threatening to attack the Muslims. He and his fellow Muslims did their best to raise the Word of Allâh high at the northen part of the Arabian Peninsula.

The Prophet ﷺ was well aware of 'Amr's skills of management. He appointed him as governor of Oman. 'Amr ﷺ established peace and justice in that land within a short period. He kept there until he received news that the Prophet ﷺ had passed away. He returned to Al-Madinah to face the dilemmas that the Muslims were entangled in after the death of the Prophet ﷺ.

A surge of apostasy began spreading throughout the Arabian Peninsula. 'Amr ﷺ was selected by Abu Bakr ﷺ as one of the army leaders to fight against the apostates. He was directed to fight a tribe called Quda'a in the northern part of the Arabian Peninsula. He undermined apostasy there and re-established the rule of Islam.

After a while, 'Amr ﷺ was commissioned by Abu Bakr ﷺ to fight the Romans in Palestine. He led an army of three thousand soldiers and was paid farewell by Abu Bakr ﷺ himself who advised him to follow the principles of Islam in his effort. He said to him:

"Be self-restrained both in privacy and in public. Allâh sees everything you do. You see that I have given you priority over other senior Companions of the Prophet ﷺ, so try to work for the Hereafter and for Allâh's sake. Care for the soldiers you lead and never make their secrets public. Be serious in your endeavours and be truthful when you meet your enemy. Do not permit any kind of deceit and punish those who deceive the Muslims."

'Amr ﷺ led the army northward. He encouraged his soldiers to be loyal to their faith and to fight their enemy as true Muslims.

'Amr ﷺ also participated as a leader of the right wing of the army in the battle of Yarmouk against the Romans and he conquered Syria with his fellow Muslims under the leadership of his friends Khalid bin Al-Waleed and Abu 'Ubaidah bin Al-Jarrah رضي الله عنهما. He dedicated most of his time for fighting evil everywhere and bringing peace and justice to every land he treaded.

The Conqueror of Egypt

'Amr ؓ continued his struggle for the sake of spreading the Word of Allâh under the rule of Abu Bakr ؓ. He spared no time for rest or pleasure.

Under the rule of 'Umar bin Al-Khattab ؓ, 'Amr ؓ was highly interested in conquering Egypt. So, he encouraged 'Umar ؓ to do so and requested him to allow him to march there, for he had known the land well before Islam when he was a trader. 'Umar ؓ permitted him to conquer Egypt and sent an army of four thousand fighters under his command. He paid him farewell with the following words:

> "March under the blessing of Allâh. I will pray to Allâh to make my choice rightful and I will inform you of my final decision. If you receive orders from me to divert attention from Egypt before you go into the land, do as I order you. However, if you receive no orders as such go on with the support and help of Allâh."

'Amr ؓ marched to Egypt until he reached Farma at the side of Syria. He surrounded the town for one month until he conquered it. He went on with his army until he reached Qantara, Salihiya and Balbees and conquered all these towns easily.

When he conquered Balbees, he caught there the daughter

of the governor of Egypt. He treated her nicely and dispatched her to her father. This act had a great effect on the governor and his people. They admired the morals of the Muslims, welcomed them and provided them with support and assistance against the Romans.

'Amr ﷺ marched toward 'Ain Shams where he lured the Romans to an open battle away from their fortresses. The Muslims fought a big battle against the Romans and finally defeated them. The remaining Roman army sought shelter in Babylon's fortress and Fayoum. So, 'Amr ﷺ continued his march, crossed the river Nile and conquered Fayoum.

A well done Job

'Amr ﷺ wrote to 'Umar ﷺ about the conquest that the Muslim army had achieved and asked him to send him more soldiers to complete his mission. 'Umar ﷺ sent him four men and told him that those four great Companions of the Prophet ﷺ were sufficient. He told him that these men were equal to four thousand soldiers. The Romans, on the other hand, gathered an army of twenty thousand soldiers under the command of Theodore. 'Amr ﷺ surrounded the fortress of Babylon's. Under the cover of darkness, Al-Zubair bin Al-Awam ﷺ, a prominent Companion of the Prophet ﷺ, with other soldiers climbed the high wall of the fortress and surprised the Romans. They opened the main gate of the fortress and let the Muslim soldiers enter the fortress. The Romans were finally conquered.

The Governor of Egypt had no choice but to ask for peace talks. Several rounds of negotiations were made between both parties. 'Amr ﷺ agreed to stop fighting and gave the people of

Egypt security for their lives, property, religion and places of worship provided that they paid *Jizya.* However, he exempted the people who embraced Islam from paying *Jizya.*

Upon his return from the camp of the Muslims, the messenger of Egypt's Governor described the Muslims to his master by saying:

> "I have seen people who like death more than they like life. They prefer humbleness over arrogance, have no avarice, sit on the ground, both rulers and subjects, so that you cannot distinguish higher class from the lower class individuals and when it is time for prayer, no one of them stays behind."

Hence, 'Amr ﷺ conquered Egypt in a short time and established Al-Fustât (an ancient Islamic city south of present day Cairo) as his base of rule. He continued his mission by marching to Alexandria and Dumyat and conquered both cities. He expelled the Romans, who treated the people of Egypt unjustly, out of Egypt forever.

'Amr ﷺ established justice and equality among the people of Egypt and treated them kindly. These acts made most of the people of Egypt accept Islam and help the Muslims against the Romans. 'Umar ﷺ the Caliph, order 'Amr to rule Egypt and to be kind to the people of the country.

'Amr did his best to develop the country and the life of the people. He built new cities, dug new streams and developed agriculture. He paved many roads and built many mosques to spread light of Islam in the country. The Muslims armies marched from Egypt in future days and conquered all the northern parts of Africa. Since he considered wealth to be a blessing from Allâh. He loved good food and good clothes.

'Amr ﷺ wrote to 'Umar ﷺ describing the land of Egypt:

"Some parts of Egypt are deserts and some other parts are covered with trees. It is divided by a blessed river that floods the land to irrigate all kinds of plants. When the flood comes, people use light boats to cross from one village to another. When the land is planted, you would see many shades and shadows. It is a blessed land."

The Governor

'Amr ﷺ settled in Egypt and adopted a policy of justice and equality among all people based on the principles of Islam. He also applied the principles of Islam to all people of Egypt on an equal basis. The Romans were not interested in developing the country or helping the Egyptians to lead an easy life. In fact, they were enslaving the Egyptians. 'Amr ﷺ ordered engineers, craftsmen and other professionals to help develop the country, especially roads, farms and water canals.

Once the Egyptians came to him and told him that they used to sacrifice a beautiful girl for the river Nile so that it may flood their lands which needed such a flooding. 'Amr ﷺ wrote to 'Umar ﷺ about this matter.

He told him that the Egyptians rely in their life on such floods. He received Umar's reply as follows:

In the Name of Allâh, the Most Gracious, the Most Merciful.

From the servant of Allâh, 'Umar bin Al-Khattab, to the Nile of Egypt.

"If you are flooding by your own will, we have no need for you; but if you are flooding by the Will of Allâh, do it in the Name of Allâh."

'Umar ﷺ ordered 'Amr ﷺ to throw the paper in the river Nile. During that very night, the Nile flooded twice the level of previous floods. The people of Egypt were very happy to save their daughters from being drowned in the river.

Sometimes sons of rulers abuse the power given to their fathers. On one occasion, one of 'Amr's sons was racing with another Egyptian young man. It happened that the Egyptian won the race. 'Amr's son became very angry and whipped the Egyptian. The Egyptian man complained to 'Umar bin Al-Khattab ﷺ. He immediately ordered for 'Amr ﷺ and his son to appear before him. Upon arriving at 'Umar's place, He asked the Egyptian to whip 'Amr's son. The Egyptian could not believe his ears. However, he whipped 'Amr's son. 'Umar ﷺ asked the Egyptian to whip 'Amr's head because his son had insulted the Egyptian by relying on the power of his father. However, the Egyptian told 'Umar ﷺ that he was satisfied. 'Umar told 'Amr ﷺ some words which are still remembered today as a basis of freedom and equality among human beings. He said:

"Since when did you enslave people while they were born free?"

'Amr ﷺ did not object to such a treatment because he knew that a Muslim should submit to the rules of Islam even though he was a governor. He made the life of the Egyptian peasants easy. He gave them the land that the Roman landlords exploited for hundreds of years. He also paved many roads and built several bridges for caravans. He also cut a canal between the river Nile and the Red Sea to enable ships to carry crops to the Arabian Peninsula.

He kept his position as the ruler of Egypt during the rule of 'Umar and 'Uthman رضي الله عنهما. He was a man of skill and intellect through which he made the land of Egypt support the other Muslims lands during hard dry years.

The Shrewd

Daring, fearless, resolute, intelligent and wise, these were some of the best qualities of 'Amr bin Al-'As ﷺ. He was a self-controlled man who never let his passions and emotions get the better of him. Purity of heart and soul distinguished him. A very pious man, he devoted his nights to prayer. At the same time he was a skillful statesman, politician and a great leader of men. He was educated in his childhood – rare in the Arabia of the times – and wrote poetry for his own entertainment but never used it to make extravagant claims and never ever did he use satire as a medium for making fun of others. Short, stocky, but well built, he was a born leader of men, a general who could get his soldiers out of any tricky situation using his experience and ingenuity.

'Amr bin Al-'Aas ﷺ had the qualities of political insight, courage, bravery, firmness of resolve, farsightedness and an ability to make quick decisions without faltering. And all these qualities he possessed to a very high degree of excellence. It was because of these virtues that in the battle of Salâsal he gained resounding victory. The Prophet ﷺ was so pleased with his triumph that he said:

"O 'Amr! Got ready for further victories."

Doubtless these words uttered by the blessed tongue of the

Prophet ﷺ were treasured with pride to the end of life of 'Amr bin Al-'Aas ﷺ as they acknowledged wholeheartedly the military services rendered by him.

And about him 'Umar bin Al-Khattâb ﷺ said:

"O 'Amr when I see your intelligence, your wisdom your understanding and your for sightedness, I feel you should have been the very first to enter into the fold of Islam."

Departure

'Amr ﷺ ruled Egypt till the 43rd year after Hijrah. He established a powerful state controlled by justice, freedom and equality.

While lying on his deathbed, he began crying. His son, Abdullah, asked him why he was crying. He replied:

"I was first disbeliever and fought hard against the Prophet ﷺ. Had I died at that time, I would have perished in the hellfire. When I embraced Islam, I felt that the Prophet ﷺ was the most lovable and most respectable man to me on the earth. If I had been asked to describe him, I would have been unable to do so because I could not look at him with full open eyes. Had I died at that time, I would have hoped to go to Paradise. I was then plighted with power and other things that I cannot say whether they were in my favour or against me. My Lord! I am not so innocent to bring my argument before myself, nor powerful to defend myself. It is only your mercy that I seek; otherwise, I have no shelter."

Some days later, 'Amr ﷺ died and was buried in Egypt after he had led a life full of activities in support of Islam and for the Islamic State.

For forty-six years, 'Amr ﷺ kept struggling hard to spread

the light of Islam. He never thought when he was in Makkah that he would be the ruler of this vast land. Had he remained a pagan, he would have vanished and never remembered by anyone. Now, all Muslims remember the shrewd and skillful leader who established firm rule of Islam in Egypt.

May Allâh forgive 'Amr ﷺ and shower His mercy on him on the Day of Judgment for he had done his best to serve the Muslim *Ummah*.